ENDORSEMENTS

★ ★ ★ ★ ★

66 Ché and Sue Ahn have been among our dearest friends and partners in ministry for over 20 years. We have ministered the gospel together all over the world. But we have covenanted together to see God heal and restore our beloved California. That's where Ché's powerful new book comes in. *Turning Our Nation Back to God* is exactly what is needed to see cities, states, and nations turn to Christ. This book will equip the believer unto that end. His biblical insight, perception of revival history, and tenderness towards the Holy Spirit all work to release what is needed for this generation to step into their purpose and destiny through a mighty outpouring of the Holy Spirit. Jesus once said regarding worship, 'The time is coming, and now is.' The same can be said here. Revival is coming. Revival is here! We must prepare our hearts, with purity and power, to steward our part in what will be the greatest revival in history. The time is now."

— Bill Johnson
Bethel Church, Redding, CA
Author of *Open Heavens* and *Born for Significance*

66 Many people in America today are deeply distressed at the state of the nation. While there are many strategies that have been posed, Ché Ahn has tapped into the central core solution with the book's subtitle—*Through Historic Revival*. If you are hungry for answers to see a changed nation, this book is a must-read."

— Dr. Cindy Jacobs
Co-Founder, Generals International

"As one who has enjoyed studying history, theology and the great revivals, I highly recommend anything written by my dear friend Ché Ahn. When Ché speaks, we need to listen. He is passionate about spiritual renewal. Ché is one of the persons God is using to bring revival to our nation."

— Dr. Jim Garlow
Co-Founder, Well Versed

"My friend Ché Ahn has once again demonstrated why the Lord has given him an apostolic mantle. The old saying is that 'those who do not know history are doomed to repeat it.' Pastor Ché redeems that phrase as he equips us to receive from and incarnate the blessings of the history of revivals and participate in the present greater work of God that is now being released. Read this and help our nation turn back to God!"

— Dr. John Jackson
President, William Jessup University
Author of Books on Personal & Cultural Transformation

"Today our nation is faced with demanding tribulations that only God can remedy. In times like these, we must turn to the inspired word of God and anointed spiritual leaders to equip ourselves for the next revival. The Holy Spirit has appointed Papa Ché to advance God's kingdom by sharing his life experience in the political arena along with biblical truths we desperately need to bring America back. This book will provide incredible guidance and wisdom to every believer that desires to be part of one of the most significant spiritual revivals of all time."

— Senator Shannon Grove *(R-Bakersfield)*
16th Senate District, California

66 My friend and brother in Christ, Dr. Ché Ahn, has followed the Lord's leading and gifted us with a book that will lead us to revival. In these pages, you will not only find a historic overview of revival in the U.S., but you will find tried and true principles that when applied, consistently and faithfully, will produce miraculous results again and again. Ché's heart for the gospel and the world that needs to hear it is clearly articulated in every chapter."

— Samuel Rodriguez
President/CEO, NHCLC
Exec. Producer, "Breakthrough" and "Flamin Hot" Movies
Author of *"Persevere With Power; What Heaven Starts,*
Hell Cannot Stop!"

66 It was said of Churchill that he used England's history like a cannon. Through that history he gave the Lion of England back its roar in that nation's darkest hour. Ché Ahn, my father in the faith, apostle of TheCall, an apostle to the nations, leader of historic revival, challenger of the governmental powers, a most courageous man of faith, in this book is like a modern-day Churchill. In using the history of revivals, their dark backdrops, their brilliant breakouts and blueprints, like a cannon Ché is giving the Church on a Hill in America back its roar in our nation's darkest hour. Is there not a history? There is one coming to America stronger than the rebellion!"

— Lou Engle
President, Lou Engle Ministries

66 Knowing our past with God helps us chart our way into the future with him. Ché Ahn's enlightening and inspiring lessons from the history of revivals offer guidance as we seek God's face for our generation now. We desperately need revival; the history of

revivals invites us to understand and fulfill the cost."

— Dr. Craig Keener
F.M. and Ada Thompson Professor of
Biblical Studies at Asbury Seminary

❝Ché has diligently poured through the Scriptures as well as the centuries of recorded history. He has identified the characteristics of previous revivals and classified the pre-actions that helped produce them. The praiseworthy service he has provided in this book can change the direction of the Church, and thus of the nation—if we will take to heart the lessons he has set forth."

— David Barton
Founder, WallBuilders

❝Ché Ahn has written a compelling book with a vision and direction for the Global Church that must be engaged. He has taken the great lessons of historical revival, from hundreds of years ago and from recent history, and propels us into the future for what we must see for revival and world harvest. Ché has carried this burden for as long as I have known him, for almost 40 years. This book is a must-read. May Christians and Messianic Jews with them be organized into the kinds of prayer for revival and harvest, for unity, from city to city, region to region, and from nation to nation. May we see transformation."

— Daniel Juster, Th.D.
Restoration From Zion

❝I had the honor of representing Pastor Ché Ahn, Harvest Rock Church, and Harvest International Ministry to challenge the unprecedented discriminatory restrictions on churches and places of worship under the guise of COVID-19. As we fought for our right to worship our Lord, and eventually won twice at the U.S. Supreme Court, I saw a man of God who was committed to follow the Lord no matter the cost. Oh, how I pray for more pastors like Ché. His fearless apostolic calling and passion for global revival and cultural transformation is evident, and it shines forth in this book. Ché has presented a fascinating review of historic revivals and a powerful way forward for revival in our generation. This book is a must-read. It will stir your heart and encourage you. Let it rain!"

— Mathew D. Staver, Esq., B.C.S.
Founder and Chairman, Liberty Counsel

God has dreams for America that aren't fulfilled yet. The best is yet to come, because we serve a King who is on the Throne and His Kingdom is ever advancing!"

— Senator Josh Hawley
Junior U.S. Senator, Missouri

This book could not be more timely! Ché Ahn reaches back into history, up into the Spirit and down into our moment of 'shaking,' and in doing so, lays out a clear path for navigating the future. It's the kind of book that's hard to put down, synthesizing so many diverse yet interesting facts and ideas that it pulled me through from start to finish. Ché has given us a Lewis and Clark guide to cross the great divide between where we are and where we really want to be. *Turning Our Nation Back to God* is indispensable reading for such a time as this."

— Dr. Lance Wallnau
Lance Learning Group
Author & Media Personality

"Ché Ahn's book, *Turning Our Nation Back to God*, inspired me greatly! In a time where so many things are uncertain and even looking hopeless for some, Ché confidently communicates the heart of God through prophetic glimpses of the great possibilities to come, a review of historical revivals and awakenings, and instruction on how to posture ourselves for the greatest display of God's presence and power ever. My expectancy, faith, and determination all exploded within me as I read this book. It is a must-read for believers in this hour!"

— Patricia King
Author, Minister, Media Producer and Host
PatriciaKing.com

"Ché Ahn is a man of faith, a courageous minister of the Gospel, and a dear friend who I deeply respect. I am grateful for his four-plus decades of faithful ministry. With his new book, I believe Ché has captured the heart of how God is preparing an unprecedented out-pouring of His Spirit among the nations of the earth. In the midst of the greatest time of escalating darkness, God will release the greatest revival in the Church (Isaiah 60:2). This book is a timely and powerful weapon in the hand of any Christ follower. I say to the Church along with Ché that it is now the time to take action and to contend for a move of God unlike anything the world has ever seen as the Holy Spirit restores the First Commandment to first place in the global Body of Christ!"

— Mike Bickle
Founder, International House of Prayer of Kansas City

"This is a MUST-READ for every pastor and spiritual leader at every level! Success requires bold courage, radical obedience and impeccable integrity. Ché Ahn has these character traits in spades. The toxic division in the Body of Christ is rampant and reflected especially between pastors with doctrinal differences. Revival requires unity and one accord despite doctrinal differences. How can you achieve that? *Read this profound book!"*

— Dr. Raleigh Washington
President & CEO, The Road To Jerusalem

For the last thirty years, Dr. Ché Ahn has been a significant apostolic voice to church, business, and political leaders on every continent. His latest book, *Turning Our Nation Back to God*, overflows with tangible hope and practical wisdom. In an easy-to-understand style, drawing principles from 500 years of revival history, it informs and challenges the reader to partner with God's purposes for this nation and for every person. Despite his responsibilities and relentless schedule, 'Papa Ché' has never stopped loving his family, befriending the ones he meets, sharing the gospel, praying for the sick and needy, and pursuing revival for his city, nation, and the nations of the earth. As you read, you will be informed, infused with apostolic hope, and activated to seek first the kingdom of God for your life and your nation."

— Charles Stock
Senior Pastor, Life Center Ministries, Harrisburg, PA

Pastor Ché Ahn is my hero. He exemplifies servant leadership and unrelenting courage. He challenged the State of California for their draconic overreach into churches and won that battle in the U.S. Supreme Court. He leads with love, driven by his passion for serving an Audience of One. Ché is a catalyst for revival, *galvanizing the Body of Christ and restoring the promise of America.* His writings are a 'must-read' for such a time as this."

— Dave Dias
Chairman of the Board, Foundations of Freedom

❝I know of no one more capable of writing this book than my friend, Dr. Ché Ahn. *Turning Our Nation Back to God Through Historical Revival* has the potential to do just that—turn our nation back to the Living God! Having experienced an outpouring of the Holy Spirit, Ché writes with conviction, presenting sobering truths to a sleeping church. God will use this book to spark fires of revival and a cultural awakening! Get this in the hands of every pastor, leader, and believer that you can!"

— Brian Simmons
Founder, Passion & Fire Ministries

❝Though we come from different backgrounds, experiences and faith traditions, I have long shared Ché Ahn's passion for revival and reformation. His thorough and detailed study of the elements and conditions God used to bring about historic revivals—including unity in the body of Christ—fills me with excitement and hope that our decades of prayers for the Greatest Awakening yet will soon be fulfilled!"

— Len Munsil, B.S., J.D.
President, Arizona Christian University

❝*Turning Our Nation Back to God Through Historic Revival* by Dr. Ché Ahn is an encouraging journey into what happens when a true revival breaks out in a church, city, region, nation, or the world. I have read scores of books on revival that are usually mostly descriptive explaining what revivals look like and how they have impacted the church and the community, even the country. Dr. Ahn's book is descriptive, but it is also prescriptive. It tells us where we are in the cycles of revival and why we are on the precipice of revival. It also gives us a prescription telling us what we need to do at this time to release the power of God for revival. I recommend *Turning Our Nation Back to God* to everyone, especially pastors, elders, deacons and all who are hungry to see God manifest his power and glory in revival."

— Dr. Randy Clark
Author of *Intimacy with God, The Healing Breakthrough,*
The Power to Heal and *There Is More*
Overseer of the apostolic network of Global Awakening
President, Global Awakening Theological Seminary

We live in extraordinarily challenging days. The Church needs multi-faceted voices, uniquely prepared by God, if we are to navigate them well. When reading this great book, I was blessed by Ché's ability to wisely interpret the past, prophetically discern the times, and instruct on moving into the future. The coming worldwide revival will demand all three. Thank You, Holy Spirit, for this book."

— Dutch Sheets
Dutch Sheets Ministries
Give Him 15: An Appeal to Heaven

No one has time to read every good book on revival. But this book demands your time. The ironclad experience of a true father of revival gives us real faith for an outpouring of the Holy Spirit. *Turning Our Nation Back to God Through Historic Revival* by Ché Ahn is a book that helps us look past the impossibilities to lay hold of a national miracle. And there is more. Wars are won by accurate maps. *Turning Our Nation Back to God* is that map. Victories come when soldiers march with total confidence. This book imparts that confidence. The enemy is defeated and nations are redeemed by wisdom and resolve. All of that and more are waiting for you in this book."

— Mario Murillo
Mario Murillo Ministries

❝We are at a most critical crossroad in our nation's history—the future and destiny of America is in the balance. Ché's powerful book *Turning Our Nation Back to God Through Historic Revival* is an essential read in order to restore our families, our cities, and our nation back to God. My dear friend Ché is an Apostle to our nation; his insights on revivals of old, his passion for a move of the Holy Spirit in our day, and his boldness to stand for righteousness in the face of all opposition has motivated Ché to author this amazing, prophetic book for our time. Now is the time for America's awakening, for the greatest revival in the history of our nation."

— Apostle Mario Bramnick
Chairman of the Board & President, Latino Coalition for Israel

❝More than most, Pastor Ché Ahn knows the need, and has the answers, to address the challenges America faces today. To turn our nation back to God, this man of God provides a blueprint. In this book, we can be pointed by the Holy Spirit in the direction that provides the solution. Reading it, following it, applying what Pastor Ché Ahn has written, truly can turn our nation back to God."

— Governor Sarah Palin
9th Governor of Alaska
Author, *Going Rogue, America by Heart*, and *Good Tidings and Great Joy*

"This book in your hands will stir the life of God in the very cells of your body. *Turning Our Nation Back to God Through Historic Revival* is not only a historic account of how God has awakened this land at times, but a modern-day account of how we must stand to keep this land awakened. Dr. Ché Ahn has masterfully communicated the need for the nation of America, as well as any other nation, to be shaken until a new glory manifests. He also reveals the need to row backwards through the waters of revival to enter the new land ahead of awakening. This is a must-read!"

— Dr. Chuck D. Pierce
President of Glory of Zion International,
Kingdom Harvest Alliance, and Global Spheres Inc.

TURNING OUR NATION BACK TO GOD

THROUGH HISTORIC REVIVAL

© 2022 by Ché Ahn

Published by Wagner Publication
11888 Gadwall Drive,
Jurupa Valley, CA, 91752

Printed in the United States of America

Cataloging-in-Publication Data is on file with the Library of Congress.
ISBN Hardcover: 978-0-9986539-6-9
ISBN Paperback: 979-8-4274918-5-3
ISBN Kindle: 978-0-9986539-9-0

Cover design by Carolyn Covell

TURNING OUR NATION BACK TO GOD
THROUGH HISTORIC REVIVAL

DR. CHÉ AHN

To my wife, Sue Ahn,
a revivalist and reformer in her own right,
especially on the family mountain.
Next to Jesus, she is the best gift that
God has given to me.

Thank you, honey, for being the best wife,
mother, and grandmother in the world.

"Many daughters have done nobly,
but you excel them all" (Proverbs 31:29).

CONTENTS

★ ★ ★ ★ ★

ACKNOWLEDGMENTS

* * * * *

First, I want to thank Jesus Christ, my Lord, who has given me the grace to be who I am.

I want to thank my spiritual son Mark Miller, who has been my editor for several years and who has done his finest work on this book project. I also want to thank Eric Metaxas for his outstanding foreword to this book. Thanks to Dr. Cindy Jacobs, Dr. Craig Keener, David Barton, and Dr. Raleigh Washington for their excellent editorial input. Additionally, I want to thank all the others who gave their endorsements for the book.

Deepest gratitude to my executive pastor Gwen Gibson and our pastors of Harvest Rock Church, who have released me to study, write, preach, and travel while they do the major work of building and maintaining a healthy local church.

I want to thank my daughter Mary Quach, former Vice President of Harvest International Ministry, and Tony Kim, Executive Director, for building HIM into an apostolic network that is now in 70 nations. We give God all the praise and glory.

I also want to acknowledge Benny Yang, who is the Vice Chancellor of Wagner University and co-publisher of Wagner Publication.

Many thanks to Rebecca Lee, my personal assistant, for her faithfulness and excellence in everything she does.

Thanks to my daughter Joy Ngu, who oversees Ché Ahn Media (CAM) and carries her father's heart. And thank you to the rest of my family, who love Jesus and have loved and honored Sue and me from the very beginning.

FOREWORD

★ ★ ★ ★ ★

"These are the times that try men's souls."

Most of us have heard that phrase, and probably more than once. Some of us have heard it so many times we couldn't begin to count how many. It's one of those phrases that is so familiar it has essentially lost its meaning. Decades ago I would use it to test out typewriters, so for me it generally had about as much resonance and power as "The quick fox jumped over the lazy dog." It had come to be so shop-worn that it was emptied of all real meaning. It's astonishing that that can happen to a sentence that once meant so much. And it was only in recent years—as our freedoms in America have come under fire—that I myself finally thought about what the sentence really meant and understood it.

The famous sentence was written by the American patriot Thomas Paine in 1776, at a time when the souls of every American patriot were being sorely tried. But so many of us have grown up almost choked with the blessings of freedom that it has been hard to imagine a world where freedom was precious, where real men and women had to fight against tyranny. Those of us who knew Paine's famous cry likely had never heard what followed that sentence. Paine goes on to say:

> *"The summer soldier and the sunshine patriot will, in this crisis, shrink from the service of their country; but he that stands by it now, deserves the love and thanks of man and woman. Tyranny, like hell, is not easily conquered; yet we have this consolation with us, that the harder the conflict, the more glorious the triumph. What we obtain too cheap, we esteem too lightly: it is dearness only that gives everything its value. Heaven knows how to put a proper price upon its goods; and it would be strange indeed if so celestial an article as FREEDOM should not be highly rated."*[1]

So here we are now, two and a half centuries later, and the words from that day of inkwells and goose quills we once again understand. Circumstances are such that the ideas of freedom and tyranny have entered our lives afresh. Suddenly we can see what it is to lose freedom, or to be on the verge of losing it, and we can see how we must fight for it—or lose it for sure.

Because of our current trials we also can see that the author of this book, my friend Ché Ahn, is a hero. He is not the summer soldier but is the sort who when difficulty came to him in his own state of California, he stood against it and fought, as he explains briefly early in this book. But what he does not say is that his actions inspired innumerable others.

It is a sobering thing to think that what we do in moments of crisis may be what causes others to act heroically. There is little doubt that Ché's heroic stance in California encouraged others in

California and elsewhere to stand and do the right thing. What we say and do affects those around us. There's no way around that. In fact what we say and do may—by God's grace—be the very straw that breaks the camel's back of evil and tyranny in our own time. Although what each of us says and does may only be a single straw, when you pile them up they may together have enough weight to crush the evil that stands against us.

So this book is another of those straws—or perhaps it's a bunch of straws. But however many straws it is, I can promise you that it is a vital addition to the growing welter of truth that is this minute in the process of putting more and more pressure on the monuments of lies and half-truths that seem to dominate the landscape of our sick culture at this time. The stories of revival that Ché tells in this book will inspire you and will help you to inspire others, and together God may use each of us to do what seems impossible.

God bless you as you read this.

— Eric Metaxas
#1 *New York Times* bestselling author and host of the
nationally syndicated *Eric Metaxas Radio Show*

PREFACE

★ ★ ★ ★ ★

Our world is in desperate need of revival. In this crucial moment in time, I am convinced that revival—true historic revival—is on God's agenda. This book is titled *Turning Our Nation Back to God Through Historic Revival* because I believe you and I are being offered a divine invitation. Right now, God is beckoning us to recognize the amazing and powerful ways that He has moved in the past so that we can act as a bridge, in the spirit, to contend for an even greater move of God in our generation. What God has done before He will surely do again.

Like the prophet Isaiah, you may be asking, "Can a nation be born in a day?" (see Isaiah 66:8). Even though great darkness surrounds us and challenges seem insurmountable, I believe we can see our nation return to God through historic revival. If we will humble ourselves and pray, seek God's face and turn from our wicked ways, God will assuredly hear from heaven, forgive our sin, and heal our land (see 2 Chronicles 7:14).

I love revival history, and my hope is that through this book, you too will value and love history, even if it was boring to you growing up. It is also my hope that you would learn the important lessons from revival history so that you can contend, pray, and position yourself to be a revivalist in your nation.

Waves of corporate revival will always come. In this book we will look at many of the different waves throughout church history. And I believe we are on the verge of the next corporate wave of revival. But you don't have to wait! You can have an exciting, dynamic relationship with Jesus now—you can experience personal revival. I believe we need to be intentional about fostering our own personal revival. We must commit to stay in the river of God. As more and more believers continually burn with the flames of personal revival, we are helping to bring about corporate revival, which in turn will impact cities, regions, and even nations.

Let me share some of my story with you. One of the reasons I personally love revival history so much is because we can learn a lot from "the good, the bad, and the ugly" that has taken place throughout church history. Renowned historian Victor Davis Hanson says, "We have a timeless connection to those who went before us—their successes and failures teach us how to succeed and avoid such failures."[2] We find a similar exhortation for the people of God in the book of Hebrews, chapters 3 and 4. In order to do proper exegesis of New Testament passages, we really need to understand the history of Judaism found in the Old Testament. Similarly, history can help us to understand and unpack Scripture with greater clarity.

Now, let me give a disclaimer: I am not a professional historian. However, I was a history major at the University of Maryland, which has one of the top history departments in the United States. In addition, and I believe by God's grace, I have had outstanding history teachers. Even when I was high on drugs, I looked forward to and went to my 11th grade history class.

Then there was Dr. Gordon Prange at the University of Maryland who was known as the expert on both World Wars and wrote the 1969 book *Tora! Tora! Tora!* on the Japanese attack on Pearl Harbor (later made into a movie in 1970). Dr. Prange was a trilingual history professor who left an indelible mark on my memory because of his incredible ability to communicate his lectures, way better than some of the preachers I respect today. I often thought that he would have been a great evangelist. I took every course he taught because he was so passionate about history, even to the point of shouting! And I can't forget Dr. Bradley at Fuller Seminary, a brilliant historian and scholar. All these history teachers were outstanding communicators who made history come alive.

I know full well that the steps of a righteous man or woman are ordered by the Lord (see Psalm 37:23), so I don't think it was just a coincidence that I was able to learn from these great professors and history teachers.

On one occasion years ago, I was spending time with one of my mentors, Winkie Pratney, who has been part of every major revival since the Jesus People movement. I asked Winkie the question, "How do you stay on fire for the Lord?" That day, Winkie gave me a key. He said that the best thing to do is to read biographies of great Christian leaders in church history. His words really stuck with me, and I made it my priority to read consistently about great leaders in Christianity, like Charles Finney, George Whitefield, the Wesleys, George Müller, and many others. I also read about outstanding leaders in secular history, including biographies of America's founding fathers, Abraham Lincoln, and so on.

Through the years, I have made it a priority to spend time *daily* in the Word and in prayer to fuel and sustain my own personal revival. I have also kept up the habit of devouring biographies, which helps me to be like the people I am reading about—to be a Christlike leader marked by morals, character, and courage. To this day, if you look at my Kindle, most of the titles on there are historical books and biographies. I love reading history in my leisure time; that's just the way I'm wired. If I hadn't been called to vocational full-time ministry, I could imagine myself teaching at a university and immersing myself in the full-time study of history.

"But Ché," you might be saying, "I'm not that into history. I'm not wired like you." Rest assured, this book is for you, too. You don't need to be a history buff to receive something powerful from revival history. Maybe you've heard it said before, history is really *His story*. Like the book of Acts, church history is about God-in-action. It is brimming over with revelations of God's faithfulness, His character, and His supernatural power. By knowing God's story—throughout the annals of time as well as in our own lives—we build up our faith in a God who works wonders.

Let me take it one step further. Our history with God prophesies into our future. Again and again in Scripture, the people of God received the emphatic mandate to continually teach their history to their children (see Exodus 13:8-9; Deuteronomy 4:9-10, 6:7, 31:19; Joshua 4:6-7; Psalm 78:3-8). Why? This was more than just passing on knowledge about the past. Dutch Sheets says it well: "When we decree what God did yesterday, it releases the same power today."[3]

David tapped into this prophetic power of knowing his history with God before taking on Goliath. When he heard formidable reports about the Philistine giant, the teenage shepherd David asked, "Is there not a cause?" (1 Samuel 17:29), which could also be translated as saying, "Is there not a *history*?" He then went on to recount how the Lord had given him victories over ferocious animals threatening his flock. David proclaimed to King Saul, "The Lord who saved me from the paw of the lion and the paw of the bear, He will save me from the hand of this Philistine" (1 Samuel 17:37). Armed with more than just a sling, David wielded history with God that prophetically empowered him to defeat Israel's most dreaded foe.

This amazing truth is expressed in both the Old and New Testaments. Revelation 19:10 concludes with the declaration, "For the testimony of Jesus is the spirit of prophecy." You see, whenever we share the stories of what Jesus has done for us, power is prophetically released for Him to do the same miracles for others. Our testimonies spark faith in a miracle-working God, the God of revival. Throughout the Old Testament, the Hebrew word for "testimony" *(eduth)* comes from the root word *ud*, meaning "to repeat" or "to do again."[4] So, a testimony carries the inherent meaning that God can—and will—do it again! That is why Revelation 12:11 says that believers will overcome the enemy "by the blood of the Lamb and by *the word of their testimony*" (NKJV).

As we journey together through revival history, I believe each account of revival will set you up to experience more of God. Stay hungry for the things of God. Keep asking for more—more of the Holy Spirit, more of His love and power, more of God's Kingdom in your life. Let's contend together for historic revival in our cities, regions, and nations until we see the promises of God fulfilled for this generation. I believe the best is yet ahead!

Dr. Ché Ahn
Pasadena, California
January 2022

INTRODUCTION

★ ★ ★ ★ ★

GLOBAL SHAKING, GREATER GLORY

The nations of the earth are being shaken like never before. This can only mean one thing: *Revival is imminent.*

If you are reading these words right now, that means you are an eyewitness to one of the most dramatic and historic seasons for the global Church. While much of what is happening around the world may seem unpredictable, God has a bulletproof plan that is currently unfolding in astonishing ways.

In fact, the prophet Haggai, around 500 years before Christ, prophesied about the very things we are living through today. In Haggai 2:7, the Word of God tells of a global shaking as well as a global revival: "'I will shake all the nations; and they will come with the wealth of all nations, and I will fill this house with glory,' says the LORD of hosts."

When God says, "I will shake all the nations," it is not hyperbole. He means *all* of them! This incredible statement is a prophetic signpost for our day, as it comes before a twofold promise: "I will fill this house with glory" (Haggai 2:7) and "The latter glory of this house will be greater than the former" (Haggai 2:9).

The First Global Shaking: WWII

In modern civilization, we have gone through two major shakings that have impacted every nation on earth. The first of these was World War II, the deadliest conflict in all of human history. Between 1939 and 1945, virtually every nation was affected by this unparalleled global war.

"World War II exhausted superlatives," writes American historian Victor Davis Hanson. "Its carnage seemed to reinvent ideas of war altogether."[5] Tragically, as many as 80 million people perished during WWII—that equates to over 36,000 casualties per day. Nations had no choice but to align either with the Allied Forces (the United States, Great Britain, and the Soviet Union) or the Axis Forces (Nazi Germany, Japan, and Italy). By the end of the war, only eight nations had successfully remained neutral: Portugal, Spain, Sweden, Ireland, Switzerland, Liechtenstein, Andorra, and the Vatican. Even when a country was not engaging in physical warfare, the economics of this global conflict had a ripple effect that left no corner of the world untouched.

This great shaking was formidable, but just as Haggai prophesied, it preceded a greater outpouring of God's glory. Each decade following World War II experienced a new move of the Holy Spirit.

In 1948, the Latter Rain Revival broke out in North Battleford,

Saskatchewan, Canada, and the following year, the Hebrides Revival spread across a group of islands off the coast of Scotland. In the year 1947, the Voice of Healing movement emerged with great healing evangelists like Oral Roberts, William Branham, Gordon Lindsay, Morris Cerullo, A.A. Allen, Jack Coe, and others. In tandem with the healing revival came the rise of evangelists Billy Graham, who was launched into international fame during a 1949 Los Angeles crusade, and Bill Bright, who founded Campus Crusade for Christ.

Ten years later, the Charismatic Renewal emerged in 1958. The decade after, in 1967, the Jesus People movement came on the scene and continued into the 70s. Then the Third Wave arrived in the early 1980s with John Wimber. Another decade later, the Toronto Blessing was sparked in 1994, followed by the Brownsville Revival in 1995. During the early days at Harvest Rock Church, we also held nightly renewal meetings at Mott Auditorium in Pasadena, California, from 1995 to 1998.

Thus, we witnessed 50 years of "jubilee" in revival taking place from the great shaking of World War II, which ended in 1945, all the way until 1995.

The Second Global Shaking: 2020

The second global shaking of modern time was the global pandemic of 2020—our generation's "perfect storm."

At the very eye of the storm was COVID-19, which blindsided over 190 nations of the world seemingly overnight. Schools and churches were mandated to close their doors along with countless family-run businesses that served as the life blood of our communities. The whole world was quarantined, an unprecedented event that had devastating repercussions. The global lockdown led to spikes in mental depression, domestic violence, alcoholism, and drug overdose, including record sales of marijuana in the state of Colorado. The death toll from COVID-19 in America was over 770,000 at the time of this writing, and over 5 million globally.

Hand-in-hand with the global pandemic came the economic meltdown. At its peak, upwards of 40 million Americans filed for unemployment relief by May 2020. In California alone, more than 16,000 businesses closed permanently due to the pandemic.[6] Even with the gradual reopening of the economy, the unemployment rate in California has remained more than double the rate preceding the pandemic.

Our nation was also shaken by the deaths of George Floyd, Ahmaud Arbery, Breonna Taylor, and others. My intent is not to debate or make a definitive commentary on the injustice of each death, but to point out the fact that these deaths impacted our society by fueling a wave of civil unrest, protests, and riots across our home-land—even a call to defund our police. There may have been more physical damage done during the 1992 riots in Los Angeles and the 1968 riots after Dr. Martin Luther King Jr.'s assassination, but in my estimation, George Floyd's death has brought about more division in our nation than any previous riots in the past. I believe that this was a significant shift in today's history and our society will never be the same.

Meanwhile, in 2020, historic wildfires burned upwards of 4 million acres of California's terrain. This unprecedented fire season surpassed the total number of acres burned in the previous three years combined. Although I am highlighting my nation and my state, every nation has gone through a shaking (see Haggai 2:6).

Top all of that off with the highly controversial 2020 election in the USA. Regardless of your political vantage point, it is clear that conservative values lost ground to the progressive Left agenda as a result of this election.

In my 48 years of walking with the Lord, I have never experienced anything like what we are seeing today. The year 2020 came and went, yet we are still seeing darkness cover the nations of the earth. What will happen as a result of all this shaking?

It is not my intent to spread a message of gloom and doom. On the contrary, I want to focus your attention on an amazing signpost of historic moves of God: *The greatest darkness precedes the greatest light of revival.*

We find this prophetic key in Isaiah 60, a well-known passage that was written around 700 years before Christ. In this chapter, Isaiah prophesies that before the great light that draws nations into God's Kingdom, there will be deep darkness over the earth. In this historic season we now find ourselves in, even as darkness tries to overcome the nations of the earth, the Lord is calling us to *rise up* and be *radiant* because His glory is rising upon His people.

> "Arise, shine; for your light has come, and the glory of the Lord has risen upon you. For behold, darkness will cover the earth and deep darkness the peoples; but the Lord will rise upon you and His glory will appear upon you. Nations will come to your light, and kings to the brightness of your rising." (Isaiah 60:1-3)

The Lawsuit: Our Fight for Religious Freedom

In 2020, darkness flooded across the entire state of California when Governor Gavin Newsom imposed the most draconian lockdown among all 50 states. As an example, 49 states had, to varying degrees, opened up in-person church services, but California was the last state to reopen—and they did only because we won a lawsuit.

As the Senior Pastor of Harvest Rock Church in Pasadena, my heart has been in Southern California since the early 1980s, sowing prayers for revival into the soil of Los Angeles along with my family, church, and dearest friends. When the pandemic hit, like so many other fellow Californians, I felt the heaviness and depression that was trying to overtake our state as the world came to a standstill. Personally, I went through my own "dark night of the soul" as I sought the Lord for some sense of clarity in the midst of overwhelming uncertainty.

As I looked to the Word of God as well as church history, I felt the Holy Spirit's assurance that this dark backdrop of the lockdown would end up serving as an opportunity for the light of God to shine all the brighter. But what I did not realize was the way that God would use this situation to reveal another area of my spiritual assignment in California—the government mountain of culture.

At the start of the pandemic in March, we heard President Trump encourage the nation to lock down for 30 days. We did not know much about the coronavirus at that point in time, but we willingly did our part to mitigate exposure to COVID-19 and complied with the quarantine guidelines. So, on March 15, we shut the doors to Harvest Rock Church and moved our services completely online.

As the lockdown kept being extended, into the month of April and then May, we witnessed the lockdown impacting countless homes and small businesses in California. At the same time, it also had a disproportionate impact on houses of worship. Churches were automatically deemed "nonessential," while abortion clinics, marijuana dispensaries, liquor stores, and later, strip clubs and casinos were allowed to keep their doors open. For our church, the decision to close our doors was sacrificial because we had to cancel our anniversary service in April, in addition to Easter Sunday and our annual conference for international leaders called Global Summit.

Soon enough, however, we started to see major discrepancies in the "data" being released about COVID-19. Gov. Newsom originally stated that out of 40 million residents of California, 22 million would potentially contract the virus and 2 million of those would die. Yet by May, my brother, Dr. Chae-woo Ahn, who is a surgeon and a member of our church, was telling me that the cases of COVID-19 being recorded in hospitals at that time were not on track to fulfill Newsom's predictions.

The pastors of Harvest Rock Church then met, and we decided to reopen in-person services at the Ambassador Auditorium on Pentecost Sunday, May 31. Right around that time, the state of California started to ease some restrictions, allowing up to 100 people to congregate in houses of worship depending on the size of the venue—but with no singing or chanting. In a spirit of honor, we encouraged anyone in our congregation with underlying conditions, high-risk individuals, and the elderly to stay home and join our services online. Most of the people who did show up were young, but we continued to mitigate by taking everyone's temperature upon entering the building, encouraging social distancing, and sanitizing everything in our building.

Meanwhile, in the wake of the George Floyd protests and riots in the late spring, state leaders consistently argued for and encouraged protestors of social justice initiatives to both congregate and chant—with no regard for social distancing or other COVID-19 precautions—often while using slogans that were degrading, defamatory, and sometimes even violent. On June 1, 2020, Gov. Newsom held a news conference in which he expressed appreciation and gratitude for the thousands of protestors gathering in the streets of California in violation of his own orders. In that press conference, Newsom explicitly encouraged the protestors to continue to flout his order: "Those that want to express themselves and have, thank you! God bless you. Keep doing it."[7] Less than a week later, on June 7, an estimated 100,000 protestors gathered in close proximity to one another in Hollywood, without any threat of criminal sanction for violating the Governor's orders.[8]

Then on July 13, Gov. Newsom made an executive order that sent California back into a total lockdown. This executive order criminalized in-person worship gatherings—whether in a church building or in a private citizen's home—as well as singing, chanting, and other means of praise. In doing so, California was mandating the most severe restrictions for churches, and these restrictions actively applied to over 90% of the population. I am sure I was not alone when I asked the question: *How can our governor publicly and unequivocally support mass gatherings for protest while simultaneously condemning and prohibiting religious worship services?*

This apparent set of double standards got me thinking about the First Amendment rights of the Church. *Where are our First Amendment rights?* In the U.S. Constitution, the First Amendment explicitly states, "Congress shall make no law respecting an establishment of religion, or prohibiting the free exercise thereof..." So, I called my attorney Mat Staver, Founder of Liberty Counsel, to receive counsel on what our course of action should be.

I told him, "You know, Mat, I am not going to lock down the church again. We are going to continue to stay open even though this new lockdown took place in July. And I just want you to cover us because I want to make sure that if I do anything that would get us into legal trouble, we will have a good attorney to support us."

Mat turned around and said, "Ché, this would be an ideal situation to sue Governor Newsom and the state of California for this egregious lockdown and violation of your First Amendment rights."

When I heard Mat say this, it was one of those moments where the Spirit of God was on me and I felt the grace to make an apostolic decision. I immediately said, "Yes." Later when I talked with my fellow pastors, elders, and church board, everyone was in agreement and stood with me in making this significant decision.

On July 17, 2020, Harvest Rock Church and our network, Harvest International Ministry, representing around 150 churches and ministries in California, filed a federal lawsuit against Gov. Newsom and California for the unconstitutional lockdown of in-person worship services. God showed us that as believers we need to take a stand for righteousness and justice in order to see His divine purposes come to pass in this crucial hour. Our rallying point was this: *The Church has been essential for 2,000 years.* Thus we went straight to the frontlines in the fight for religious liberty in America.

On August 13, I received a dark and disturbing letter from the city prosecutor of Pasadena. The letter threatened to put me in jail for one year and fine me, the church, staff, and every attendee $1,000 per service since our reopening on May 31—which would have amounted to millions of dollars in fines. Even more troubling, the letter asserted that they reserved the right to arrest every church member attending these services.

All of that shocked me, in light of all the ways we have served and blessed our city over the years. The irony is that California officials were letting prisoners out of jail because of the threat of COVID-19 spreading through overcrowded prisons, but they wanted to arrest law-abiding citizens who were exercising their First Amendment right to assemble and simply worship Jesus. Righteous anger rose up within me as I thought to myself, *This is madness.* It struck me that we have come to an Isaiah 5:20 period in time, where people are calling evil "good" and light "darkness."

Despite the darkness we were facing, the Spirit of God only strengthened our resolve to move forward. After we officially sued Gov. Newsom, the local news media showed up at our church, and hate mail came pouring in: "You are one selfish pastor." "You hate your church." "You are killing your church." What grieved me—

more than the hateful emails or even the prospect of facing jail-time—was to see some of the members of our church leave because of the stand we took. These were people who are near to my heart. A long time ago, I made the resolution found in Galatians 1:10: "… If I were still trying to please people, I would not be a bond-servant of Christ." I am here first to love God with all of my heart, mind, soul, and strength, and second to love my neighbor as myself (Mark 12:29-31). In this situation, loving my neighbor meant to do what is right, and I was convicted that we needed to open up our church and stay open.

Our lawsuit began with a request for an immediate injunction to protect me from being arrested, but the district court denied that request. Next, we went to the Ninth Circuit Court of Appeals, which also shot us down. It is interesting to note that the Ninth Circuit is the most extreme liberal court in California, as most of the judges were appointed by Presidents Obama and Clinton. In fact, some 80% of decisions made by the Ninth Circuit end up being overturned by the Supreme Court, which has not always been conservative like it is today. (On a side note, this goes to show that elections do have consequences. Probably the most significant thing that President Trump did was nominate three Supreme Court justices that were constitutionalists as well as almost 300 federal judges!)

Undeterred, we appealed to the U.S. Supreme Court, not knowing whether our case would be chosen for consideration. We watched as the High Court ruled in favor of synagogues and Catholic churches fighting a similar battle in New York City, in the cases *Roman Catholic Diocese of Brooklyn v. Cuomo* and *Agudath Israel v. Cuomo*. Shortly after Thanksgiving, we received a phone call saying the Court would also weigh in on our case.

On December 3, 2020, the Supreme Court convened and granted our request for a temporary injunction. This decision was intended to send a powerful message to the lower courts affirming that churches can meet without fear of being reprimanded or arrested. The problem was that the courts in California are out of control. The judges who were assigned to our case completely disregarded the Supreme Court's admonishment and proceeded to rule against us.

Again, we appealed our case. On February 5, 2021, the Supreme Court ruled in a 6-3 vote in our favor and ended the ban on indoor church services in California. This was long after the other 49 states had reopened for in-person worship. The High Court gave its 6-3 decision as a road map for the lower courts to follow. Unfortunately, the lower courts again fought against our cause.

So, the battle continued. By the grace of God, we persevered in this prolonged ordeal, knowing that "our struggle is not against flesh and blood," but we were in a spiritual battle (Ephesians 6:12).

Then on April 9, we had the most significant breakthrough: The Supreme Court ruled 5-4 in favor of small groups and Bible studies being permitted to meet in homes in California. What a glorious day! That date, April 9, holds special significance as the 115th anniversary of the Azusa Street Revival and the 76th anniversary of Dietrich Bonhoeffer's martyrdom standing against the totalitarianism of Hitler. After that ruling, the Attorney General phoned our attorney with the long-awaited news that it was time to settle our case.

Finally, on May 17, 2021—after nearly a yearlong battle—our lawsuit reached a landmark settlement in our favor. This ruling completely reversed the last discriminatory restrictions against churches in California. Furthermore, it imposed a permanent injunction against our governor and any future governors from locking down the church in any situation, whether a pandemic or another crisis, and if they do, they will be in contempt of court. The exclamation point was that our attorney Mat Staver and his law firm, Liberty Counsel, was awarded $1.35 million in settlement for legal fees incurred during this lawsuit!

Ultimately, this historic settlement was a victory for the Church in America. This case will act as a precedent not only in our state but also in our nation. In the end, it took multiple "rebukes" from the Supreme Court and a recall process before Gov. Newsom relented and gave the Church what should have been our First Amendment rights from the beginning. It is very likely we would still be in lockdown if we hadn't taken legal action and sued our governor. We are incredibly grateful to Mat Staver and Liberty Counsel for their relentless support and fierce determination. Most of all, we give God all the glory for moving mightily in this historic season!

A Season of Greater Glory

We are in a truly historic season, a new era in the spirit. Despite the increase in darkness around us, the Church is being rallied to shine the light of Christ with even greater intensity. Excitement is in the air because this is the season for historic revival. As 2020 was just about to dawn, I felt the Spirit of God saying that 2020 was the beginning of a Great Revival and that this will be a decade of Great Harvest in America. If "the latter glory of this house will be greater than the former" (Haggai 2:9), what will it look like?

Because of the magnitude of what God is doing in our day and age, it is necessary for the Church to be spiritually discerning like the sons of Issachar, who understood the times that they were living in and knew what course of action to take accordingly (1 Chronicles 12:32). You wouldn't wear summer clothes in wintertime or take a snowboard with you to the beach. In the same way, it is not the time for the Church to just sit back and let the world call the shots. It is time for laborers to charge into the fields that are ripe for harvest!

PART 1:

LESSONS LEARNED FROM HISTORIC REVIVALS

★ ★ ★ ★ ★

Chapter 1

THE DARKEST HOUR PRECEDES THE GREATEST REVIVAL

★ ★ ★ ★ ★

I f the world around you is looking dark, just hold on—because God is on the move.

The entire globe was hit hard by the year 2020. Young or old, poor or rich, we all have been going through a season of unparalleled shaking, uncertainty, and extreme darkness spreading across the nations of the earth. Some of the darkness and fear have been manmade, for example, politicizing the pandemic for Leftist gain. But God, who rules over the earth, is using this pandemic for His glory. In the midst of the darkness, here is a promise that you can hold onto: *The darkest hour always precedes the greatest light of revival.*

The Word of God encourages us in Isaiah 60:2-3, "For behold, darkness will cover the earth and deep darkness the peoples; but the Lord will rise upon you and His glory will appear upon you. Nations will come to your light, and kings to the brightness of your rising." Wherever you see darkness in the world, I believe God is preparing for great light to break forth. It is against this stark backdrop of darkness that God's light will shine the brightest as He brings revival to a lost and hurting world.

I have read biblical scholars commenting that Isaiah 60 is a prophecy about the post-exilic return of Israel to their homeland after spending 70 years in Babylon. In 586 BC, Nebuchadnezzar destroyed Jerusalem and the Temple, taking the Jewish people into captivity. Isaiah and Jeremiah prophesied about the return of God's people to the land that God had given them, and the prophecies appear to say that they would return to the former glory of what was experienced in 2 Chronicles 5. As Solomon brought up the Ark of the Covenant to the dedication of the Temple, the glory of God came in such a manifest way that the priests could no longer stand up, because the Temple was filled with a cloud of His glory (2 Chronicles 5:11-14).

Similarly, Haggai's prophecy about the "latter glory of this house" seemed to indicate that the second Temple, built under Zerubbabel, would experience even greater glory than Solomon's Temple. Historically, that did not happen. The glory of the Lord did not come to the Temple under Zerubbabel, Haggai, or Ezra the way it manifested in 2 Chronicles 5.

The point I want to make is that prophecies in Scripture often have a number of applications, and there are different layers of interpreting the prophetic. So, while there is no question about Isaiah 60 prophesying the post-exilic return of Israel, I believe the ultimate fulfillment of this prophecy is for the end times—*for us*—when the glory of Jesus Christ will shine with greater clarity and power than in any other time in history. Isaiah 60:1 says, "Arise, shine; for your light has come, and the glory of the Lord has risen upon you." We know that Jesus is the Light of the world, and He also calls you the light of the world (see John 8:12 and Matthew 5:14). I believe Isaiah 60 is talking about when the Messiah, Jesus, would come in fulfillment of all the Old Testament prophecies.

When we read the promise in Isaiah 60:3, "Nations will come to your light, and kings to the brightness of your rising," I don't see that as an accurate description of what happened in Israel's history. The nation of Israel was under the reign of other nations for centuries. Even after the Babylonian exile, Israel was still a vassal state under the Persians, followed by the Syrians, the Greeks, and then the Romans until the time of Jesus. Therefore, I see that as another aspect of the prophecy extending to our time in history, when nations will come to the light of salvation in Jesus Christ.

This biblical principle of darkness preceding light is seen again and again throughout revival history. Let's take a look at some of the key examples that I pray will spark hope in us as we anticipate the light of revival breaking forth today.

The Black Death, Then the Reformation

The first example of a demonstrably dark season is the Black Death of 1348. The Black Death or Bubonic Plague was caused by a bacterium, not a virus like the coronavirus, that was usually transmitted through the bite of an infected rat flea. Originating in China in 1331, the plague was absolutely devastating to the human population. When the Silk Road opened up trade from China to Europe, the shiploads carrying goods would come to Europe, but they also carried rats and fleas that were then able to disperse into densely populated cities.

An estimated 25 million people died from the Black Death, much more than any virus to date (as of this writing, over 5 million have died because of COVID-19). The plague has persisted in intermittent epidemics over the past 700 years, and to this day, there are pockets of the disease appearing in the Congo, other parts of Africa, and Peru. We read in history how the Black Death devastated Europe, and yet during the time when this plague came to a peak, God started to raise up reformers.

In the middle of the 14th century, there arose the "morning star" of the English Reformation, John Wycliffe (1320-1384). A brilliant Oxford professor and Roman Catholic priest, Wycliffe is best known today for creating the first complete English translation of Scripture, now known as the Wycliffe Bible. Even though he belonged to the Catholic Church, Wycliffe ruffled feathers around him with his strong convictions. He preached the message of justification by grace through faith and acknowledged the Bible as the only source of truth. Likewise, he proclaimed that the pope was not infallible, and he called out the unbiblical teachings about purgatory, the veneration of relics, and the worship of saints. Wycliffe also led a band of evangelists called the Lollards who radically preached the gospel to people across all levels of society.[9]

One of Wycliffe's disciples, Jan Hus of Bohemia (1369-1415), picked up the reformer's mantle and kept up the momentum in the spirit. Like Wycliffe, Hus was an academic, serving as a professor at the University of Prague, and a radical preacher of the gospel. He went against the grain by delivering his sermons in Czech, the language of the people, instead of Latin. He also placed supreme importance on the Bible and Christ's role as head of the Church. Due to his determination and controversial convictions, Hus was excommunicated. Later he was betrayed by the Holy Roman Emperor Sigismund, condemned as a heretic at the Council of Constance, and burned at the stake after refusing to recant his beliefs.[10] Hus became a martyr for his faith, and his death created shockwaves among Bohemian faith communities that would continue the struggle for a brighter future.

Another voice crying out for reformation was Girolamo Savonarola (1452-1498), a Dominican monk in Italy who moved in signs and wonders. Savonarola served as Prior of the San Marco convent in Florence, where revival swept many into the Kingdom of God during the last four years of Savonarola's life. His messages shook listeners with "such terror and alarm, such sobbing and tears, that people passed through the streets without speaking...."[11] This Italian reformer also had a tremendous influence on the famed artist Michelangelo, who sat under his teaching, and many believe Savonarola was the catalyst for the Renaissance emerging in Italy during his lifetime. Ultimately, Savonarola's radical disposition would lead him down the martyr's path, as he was denounced as a heretic, publicly hanged, and burned.

Thus, during this darkness, reformers arose burning with the light of revival. This momentum culminated in the Protestant Reformation that was sparked on October 31, 1517. On that day, the German monk Martin Luther nailed his 95 Theses on the Wittenberg church door, addressing problems and excesses in the Church of his day.

Even though there was authentic ministry taking place in the Church, superstition was widespread at that time. One of the things that the Catholic Church taught and backed up was that you could buy a relic—for example, a small piece of wood supposedly from the Cross of Jesus—to be healed of the Black Plague. In fact, so many of these relics were sold that if you put them all together, it would form an entire forest, not just a single tree. It was a total scam, and the Catholic Church was making money by taking advantage of the ignorance and lack of education of the everyday churchgoer.

Indulgences were another area of contention. If someone in your family died of the Black Plague and they were believed to be in purgatory, the Church alleged that you could reduce the time your relatives spent in purgatory by giving an offering, an "indulgence," to the Church. Those are some of the practices that Martin Luther denounced as unbiblical when he published his 95 statements.

A true trailblazer and influencer, Luther ran forward with the blazing torch of God's truth that we are forgiven and justified by grace through faith alone. Thus, the Reformation began, leading to the birth of the Protestant Church.

The Great Plague, Then the First Great Awakening

Fast forward to the 17th century, and we find another extremely dark chapter in history that preceded a major move of God. Lasting from 1665 to 1666, the final major epidemic of the bubonic plague to occur in England was known as the Great Plague. Within a matter of 18 months' time, the Great Plague killed an estimated 100,000 people in London alone—almost a quarter of the city's population.[12] Around the same time, gin came onto the scene, creating a wave of debauchery and destructive repercussions. The Gin Age (described in detail in Chapter 7) led to spikes in poverty, crime, and prostitution. Due to the "Gin Craze" in the early 1700s, England became a nation of alcoholics.

The land was steeped in darkness when revival broke out in 1738. On December 31, 1738, a group of 60 believers met for an all-night prayer meeting on Fetter Lane in London. Some from the Oxford-based "holy club" were present, including George White-field and John and Charles Wesley. As they prayed into the new year, the Holy Spirit fell on those gathered there and marked them with powerful encounters into the wee hours of the morning. John

Wesley recorded in his journal on January 1, 1739: "About three in the morning, as we were continuing instant in prayer, the power of God came mightily upon us, insomuch that many cried out for exceeding joy, and many fell to the ground. As soon as we were recovered a little from the awe and amazement at the presence of his Majesty, we broke out with one voice, 'We praise thee, O God, we acknowledge thee to be the Lord.'"[13]

A tremendous harvest ensued as Whitefield and the Wesleys preached across England in the days to follow. Thousands started to gather as these energetic evangelists open-air preached, which was unheard of in their day. In England around 1.25 million people came to Christ between the years 1738 and 1791. Whitefield also took the revival fires to America, where thousands came to the light of Jesus Christ. In a single year of itinerant ministry, Whitefield traveled multiple thousands of miles on horseback going up and down the Atlantic coast, often preaching three times a day. In both America and Great Britain, the First Great Awakening had enormous ripple effects on the Church and society at large.

The Second Great Awakening

In every chapter of church history, there is always a remnant contending for revival, especially in times of darkness. So, too, in America's fledgling colonies there was a remnant that was believing God for another move of the Holy Spirit. For example, out of the 56 founding fathers who signed the Declaration of Independence in 1776, all were either Evangelical Christians or had a background with prominent Christian values (none of whom were deists).[14] We must also realize that our democracy was not totally established at this time, and we know there were believers praying that God would continue to bless and build this nation leading up to the War of 1812.

And God answered their prayers when the next Great Awakening broke out in 1801. One of the vessels used by God to spark revival was a man named James McGready. This Methodist minister's claim to fame was that he was an ugly, very homely man. So, when people heard that McGready could preach, they wanted to hear what he had to say! McGready was indeed an incredible preacher, and the spirit of revival was on him.

Typical of the outdoor meetings of Whitefield during the First Great Awakening, McGready started to hold open-air meetings in Cane Ridge, Kentucky, in 1801. These "camp meetings" started to gain momentum as thousands came during the summer months and camped out to hear not only McGready preach but also other Baptist, Presbyterian, and Methodist preachers that had been invited. These daily gatherings grew to as many as 30,000 people, which is astounding when you realize that in those days Kentucky's largest town was home to less than 2,000 inhabitants.

The Spirit of God fell on these meetings and many attendees experienced spiritual manifestations, including physical shaking. It was told that one woman who had pins to hold her hair up started to jerk so much that her pins went flying like missiles. In other cases, it was reported that the jerking of bodies created a sound that was louder than a horse whip. Some of the same manifestations that were noticeable in the Toronto Blessing of the 1990s took place during the Cane Ridge revival at the start of the 1800s. That revival spread through Charles Finney and others like the Methodist circuit riders who preached all throughout the United States.

Another notable event was in August of 1806, as five students from Williams College in Massachusetts were meeting in a grove of maple trees. When a thunderstorm suddenly hit, they saw a stack of hay and ran under it to take cover. Under the haystack, they made a vow to do all they could do to reach the unreached nations of the earth with the gospel. Those were the humble beginnings of the modern mission movement that eventually led to the creation of the American Board of Commissioners of Foreign Missions, the United Foreign Missionary Society, the American Bible Society, and later the Student Volunteer Missionary Movement under the influence of D.L. Moody, A.T. Pierson, and John R. Mott. Their battle cry was the evangelization of the world in one generation.

A new surge of revival came in 1857-1858 with the Prayer Revival that broke out in New York. On September 23, 1857, Jeremiah Lanphier, a New York businessman who was saved under Charles Finney's ministry, started a prayer meeting at the North Church, a Dutch Reformed Church on Wall Street. Within just six months' time, 10,000 New York businessmen were gathering every single day to pray.[15] The ensuing revival brought in around 2 million new believers, many of whom lived in the North and were abolitionists. In the wake of the Civil War (1861-1865), the North's victory over the South led to the abolition of slavery in the United States. The wave of revival continued under the leadership of evangelist Dwight L. Moody into the later decades of that century. (You can read more about the 1857 Prayer Revival in Chapter 6.)

The Turbulent 60s and the Jesus People Movement

There are so many other examples we could consider throughout the annals of history. A time period close to home for me was the turbulent 1960s leading into the Jesus People movement.

For those Baby Boomers who grew up in my generation and lived through the era, you'll recall how the 1960s were defined by huge countercultural shifts and widespread unrest. The Cold War and threat of communism set a sobering backdrop for the rise of the hippie drug culture and the sexual revolution of Haight Ashbury. Meanwhile, blood was shed on the streets of America as black citizens continued the intense uphill battle for civil rights. The heart of the nation was shaken by the assassinations of Martin Luther King Jr., President John F. Kennedy, and Senator Robert Kennedy.

To top it all off, the Vietnam War was also raging on, with an increasing number of American casualties and no resolution in sight. Consequently, our nation experienced significant social upheaval and disillusionment as war protests became widespread. In 1972, I joined ranks with those protesting the war in Vietnam. Looking back on it now, I didn't really know what I was doing; I was just 16 years old at the time. But anti-war sentiments could be found far and wide, ranging from speeches at college campuses, to demonstrations at the Lincoln Memorial, to hit new songs on the airwaves.

Not a lot of young people today realize that the protests during the 60s were a lot worse than what we have recently witnessed in America. The 1968 Democratic Convention in Chicago turned into riots, and TVs all across the homeland displayed the violence that ensued. Two years later, the Ohio National Guard was called into Kent State University, where they shot at student protesters, leaving four dead. Can you imagine the outrage that would erupt if Americans witnessed something like that happening today? Yet all of that happened in my generation.

The 1960s were unmistakably a very dark time in our nation's history. But then in 1967, the Jesus People movement broke onto the scene. The light and hope of the gospel swept across America as millions of young people fell in love with Jesus and abandoned their old lifestyles. I thank God that I was one of the hordes of hippies that came to know His transformational love and received new life in Christ during the wave of the Jesus People movement. (I share more about this move of God in Chapter 6, "The Harvest Comes In.")

Greater Things to Come

I believe we are coming into another season of revival that is going to eclipse the Jesus People movement. We are going to experience greater glory, greater presence, greater deliverance, and greater salvation. No matter how dark it may seem in your surroundings, let hope arise in your heart—because the light of Jesus Christ is greater than any darkness, and His glory will assuredly rise upon *you*!

Chapter 2

THE CHURCH MUST GO BACKWARD BEFORE IT CAN GO FORWARD

★ ★ ★ ★ ★

The 20th century revivalist Vance Havner once said, "What we call revival is simply New Testament Christianity, the saints going back to normal." It might seem counterintuitive at first, but we must return to God's standard before we can advance in the spirit. Revival history shows us that the Church must go backward before it can go forward.

Every time revival breaks out, it involves believers going back to the Early Church and restoring a truth from God's Word that was lost through religion. This is all to move forward with the new move of God. Fred and Sharon Wright, in their book *The World's Greatest Revivals*, record that each of the major revivals in church history "emphasizes essential truths about the nature and purposes of God that have been ignored, discarded, or lost by successive generations of professing believers and well-meaning church leaders and theologians."[16] When people are desperate for God and return to the truth of His Word, the resulting "proclamation of rediscovered truth" acts as a catalyst for a fresh outpouring of God's presence, leading to revival.[17]

In the apostle Peter's Pentecostal sermon, Acts 3:19 includes a call to return to God preceding times of revival: *"Repent therefore, and turn back,* that your sins may be blotted out, that *times of refreshing* may come from the presence of the Lord."* Verses 20-21 then talk about how this is part of restoring every truth from God's Word: "…and that He may send Jesus Christ, who was preached to you before, whom heaven must receive *until the times of restoration of all things,* which God has spoken by the mouth of all His holy prophets since the world began."

Here we notice the pattern that God's people must turn back to His truth before we can move forward and receive times of spiritual refreshing. Throughout church history, every move of the Spirit restored a truth that was already there in the Word of God, just waiting for the Church to embrace it and walk in its fullness.

Most Evangelicals will confess that they believe the Bible is the inspired, inerrant Word of God. They will say they believe in the whole Bible, but do they really? For example, there are numerous pastors who preach that spiritual gifts like healing and working of miracles (see 1 Corinthians 12:8-12) are not for today. We even have a theological term for these Evangelical believers; they are cessationists. They believe the charismatic gifts ceased when the canon of Scripture was closed. We know that this is not true when we read how healings and miracles continued throughout church history,[18] but the doctrine of the spiritual gifts was restored during the Azusa Street Revival of 1906. Let's look at other truths that the Holy Spirit restored through historic revival.

Back to the Basics: Martin Luther

Through the Protestant Reformation starting in October 1517, the Church had to go back to basic doctrines in Scripture before it could move forward with the fresh move of God. These basic biblical teachings included Martin Luther's affirmation of justification by grace through faith alone. This is something that we take for granted today, but back in Luther's day, this was not preached in the Catholic Church.

When Luther issued his 95 Theses written in Latin, he was making public a series of strong declarations to affirm sound theology and refute erroneous biblical interpretation. The most well-known of these theses spoke against indulgences, tax laws, and a teaching by the Pope that said if you gave money to the church, you could reduce your time in purgatory—not get to Heaven, just reduce your time in purgatory.

Martin Luther rejected this teaching as nonsense. It had absolutely no basis in Scripture. The Bible, on the contrary, declares that we are forgiven by God's grace and freely receive the gift of eternal life (see Ephesians 2:8-9). As he challenged the unbiblical teachings of his time, Luther captured the spirit of Isaiah 55:1: "Come, all you who are thirsty, come to the waters; and *you who have no money*, come, buy and eat! Come, buy wine and milk *without money and without cost.*"

Another Catholic doctrine that Luther refuted was the doctrine of infallibility. This belief validated anything that the Pope taught as truth, even when it was erroneous teaching. To counter the doctrine of infallibility, Luther affirmed the doctrine of *sola scriptura*. Scripture alone, God's Word in the Bible, is the only infallible source of authority for Christ followers.

After Luther released his 95 Theses, copies were soon made and spread abroad all throughout Germany. That marked the beginning of the Protestant Reformation, which would play an enormous role in shaping modern history as we know it. Thus, to go forward with the move of God emerging in his day, Martin Luther had to go back to the foundational truths from the Word of God.

The Return to Believer's Baptism: The Anabaptists

Right as the Protestant Reformation was taking flight, a distinct movement in Europe initiated another return to the Word of God. In 1525 the Anabaptists (literally meaning "those who baptize again") came on the scene in Zurich, Switzerland, among leaders such as Conrad Grebel and Felix Manz. While they were contemporaries of Martin Luther and the Swiss reformer Ulrich Zwingli, the Anabaptists were convicted that the measures taken by Luther and Zwingli were not radical enough. An even greater reformation was needed, they contended.[19]

While the Anabaptists held to a variety of convictions, their stance on baptism became characteristic of the movement. Infant baptism was one of the main practices that they rejected. In contrast to the longstanding tradition, Anabaptists held that a person is to be baptized in water when he or she professes faith in Jesus Christ. This requires conscious action on behalf of the believer (see Acts 8:36-37), not a ceremonial act in which a baby only passively participates. Thus, anyone who joined the ranks of the Anabaptists was rebaptized.

Through the Anabaptist movement, God was moving to restore truth from His Word and revive His Church. Charles P. Schmitt writes that the Anabaptists were active participants in the Spirit's work "restoring yet more of the simplicities of the Christian life: believer's baptism, Spirit-filled church life… living a life of non-violence, and the community of goods."[20] The Spirit was expressly at work among the Anabaptist community, to the extent that dancing, speaking in tongues, and falling under the power of God were common occurrences in those circles.

The movement gave way to two prominent branches: the Mennonites and the Hutterites. The Mennonites got their name from Menno Simons, a priest from Holland, and the Hutterites were named after Jacob Hutter, a hat maker from Tyrol (modern-day northern Italy). The Anabaptist movement did not progress, however, without opposition.

Like Martin Luther, who was both excommunicated and banned from the Holy Roman Empire, many of those who subscribed to the Anabaptists' beliefs experienced severe persecution. Some were tortured, some were hanged, and others, like Hutter, were burned alive because of their convictions. Through their sacrificial obedience to God, the Anabaptists helped restore truth from God's Word so their generation could advance into the fresh move of the Spirit.

The Return to Personal Holiness: John Wesley

Fast forward to the 18th century, and another important restoration of biblical truth took place during the First Great Awakening. Thanks to the influence of John Wesley, a founder of Methodism, the Church at large answered the call to return to personal holiness. Schmitt explains, "No movement in the restoration of the apostolic church on the earth is more impressive than early Methodism with its quest for the inner fire of the Holy Spirit, its deeper life 'cell-group' concept, and its evangelical social revolution. And no leader stands more impressive than its stilted, abrupt apostle, John Wesley of Epworth,

England...."[21]

Raised as one of 19 children, John Wesley grew up in a home of pronounced faith, morals, and discipline. While studying at Oxford, Wesley joined the "holy club" that his brother Charles had pioneered. This was a society in which each member made a vow to live a life of holiness—something that would mark Wesley for years to come. They also held a daily Bible study, committed themselves to prayer, took Communion every week, and regularly visited prisons.[22]

In May 1738, John Wesley had a deeply personal encounter with the Spirit of God that marked a pivotal point in his life. By the following year, another former "holy club" member, George Whitefield, started reaching thousands of England's poor with the gospel in his avant-garde outdoor sermons. In response to Whitefield's urgent and energetic exhortations, many dramatic conversions were taking place. Wesley, though initially reluctant, agreed to take up Whitefield's ministry in Bristol when Whitefield departed for America.

The first time Wesley open-air preached, the Holy Spirit fell. People started to weep and fall under the power of God. There were great manifestations of the Holy Spirit as well as demonic manifestations and deliverance. The fruit that Wesley saw made him a believer in open-air meetings, and he followed in Whitefield's wake as a firebrand preacher who took the English countryside by storm. Thus, the First Great Awakening was on.

John Wesley's personal life and leadership were marked by a remarkable sense of disciplined or methodical practices. This was made evident by the fact that Wesley and his followers earned the label "methodists" from critics, though they would actually go on to embrace the name with gusto.

In June 1744, the first Methodist annual conference was held as John and Charles Wesley, along with eight others, agreed upon points of doctrine and practice for the emerging movement. In addition to affirming justification by faith and assurance of salvation, they also underscored "how important it was for all believers to advance in holiness toward perfection in Christ."[23] John Wesley's ministry would continue to emphasize "sanctification by faith in the fire of the Spirit of God" for years to come.[24]

During the mid-1700s, the doctrine of Christian perfection would attract controversy. While others strayed from Scripture in their teachings, Wesley went back to the Bible as he taught about the sanctifying work of the Holy Spirit: "Christians are called to love God with all their heart, and to serve him with all their strength; which is precisely what I apprehend to be meant by the scriptural term perfection."[25] Wesley professed that the Christian faith isn't just about being born again but about growing in personal holiness. He taught on the importance of sanctification as manifested by "the humble, gentle, patient love of God and man ruling all the tempers, words, and actions, the whole heart by the whole life."[26]

Another truth that was restored during Wesley's time was the Church's call to fulfill the Great Commission: "Go, therefore, and make disciples of all the nations, baptizing them in the name of the Father and the Son and the Holy Spirit, teaching them to follow all that I commanded you…" (Matthew 28:19-20).

As an itinerant preacher, "Wesley was indefatigable. His energy was prodigious," writes Vishal Mangalwadi. "He got up each morning at four and preached his first sermon most mornings at five."[27] In his lifetime, Wesley preached over 45,000 sermons, frequently to crowds exceeding 20,000 people. Nothing could stop his passionate pursuit of the Great Commission. "Wesley traveled a quarter of a million miles on horseback, in all weather, night and day, up and down and across England, on roads that were often dangerous and sometimes impassable."[28]

John Wesley also raised up 1,500 traveling preachers who continued to expand the reach of the gospel well beyond his lifetime. By the time of Wesley's death, the Methodist movement was comprised of approximately 140,000 members.[29] Today, it numbers over 40 million worldwide.

Holy Spirit Baptism and Spiritual Gifts

During the 19th century, God was preparing His Church to restore another truth from His Word, this time focusing on the work of the Holy Spirit. Great leaders like Charles Finney, Asa Maham, and Thomas Upham set the stage for the ensuing Holiness revivals in the latter half of that century. "It was these men, among others, who inaugurated the great American Holiness movement of the 1800's with its strong emphasis on a definite conversion experience, a specific baptism in the Holy Spirit, and heart purity...."[30] There also arose Dwight L. Moody, A.J. Gordon, Charles Spurgeon, and Maria Woodworth-Etter, who experienced their own personal "Pentecost," preached about the baptism of the Spirit, and ushered in corporate revival during the mid to late 1800s.

By the dawn of the 20th century, the Lord was stirring up a strong hunger in His people for more of the Spirit. The year 1900 saw a breakout of the Holy Spirit and spiritual gifts in Topeka, Kansas, when Charles Parham laid hands on a woman and she began to speak in tongues. This outbreak eventually led to the Azusa Street Revival of 1906. At Azusa Street, the truth was restored that God doesn't just want to save you—He wants to baptize you in the Holy Spirit and power. With the baptism of the Holy Spirit also came the recognition of spiritual gifts.

William Seymour, one of Parham's students, was at the forefront of the Azusa Street Revival. In my estimation, Seymour was one of the greatest apostles in church history. More was accomplished to advance the Kingdom through this man than any other person apart from the apostle Paul. By the way, Seymour was blind in one eye, but he could *see more* of the Spirit than anyone else (pun intended). God used this man in a mighty way to spark the Third Great Awakening and the spread of Pentecostalism.[31]

The fire of Azusa Street first spread throughout Los Angeles, then to other states, and then internationally. In the fall of 1906, 38 individuals were commissioned by the Azusa Street Mission as missionaries with both international and domestic trajectories. By 1908, revival centering around the work of the Holy Spirit was taking place in 50 nations—with no signs of slowing down. This move of God was so explosive that by 1914 the Pentecostal movement had amassed members in every city in America with a population of over 3,000 people and every region around the world.[32]

Today, the movement of "Spirit-empowered Christians"— including Pentecostals, Charismatics, and others sharing a belief in the baptism of the Holy Spirit—accounts for one in every four believers around the world, or 644 million people.[33]

The Restoration of Fivefold Ministry

Over the course of the last 70 years or so, the Body of Christ has seen the progressive restoration of the ministry gifts that God gave His people to operate in. Bishop Bill Hamon teaches in his eye-opening book *The Day of the Saints* that God has been restoring the full operation of the fivefold ministry.

Leading into the 1950s the office of the evangelist was emerging. In the 1960s the office of the charismatic pastor was being restored. In the 1970s it was the office of teacher. Then in the 1980s the office of prophet was restored, and in the 1990s, the office of apostle. Each of these steps in restoring the fivefold has accompanied moves of the

Holy Spirit.

In the late 1940s and early 1950s, I believe God restored the office of evangelist in the Church. In the fall of 1949, the young evangelist Billy Graham scheduled a three-week crusade in Los Angeles that ended up lasting a total of eight weeks. Over 350,000 people attended the meetings and upwards of 3,000 got saved, thus marking Graham's entrance into the international spotlight.[34] In 1951, Bill Bright founded what would later become the world's largest international Christian organization, Campus Crusade for Christ, on the campus of UCLA. During this same time frame, many healing evangelists were raised up, including T.L. Osborn, Morris Cerullo, and Oral Roberts in Tulsa, Oklahoma.

Then came the charismatic pastors. From the year 1958 flowing into the 1960s, the Charismatic Renewal gave rise to many amazing pastors from various movements. Larry Christenson, of the Lutheran charismatic movement, and Gerald Derstine, a Charismatic Mennonite, are just two examples. Another major influence during this time frame was Dennis Bennet, an Anglican priest at St. Mark's Episcopal Church in Van Nuys, California, who was baptized in the Holy Spirit in 1959 and later made waves with the bestseller *Nine O'Clock in the Morning* (referring to Peter's message in Acts 2).

Next in line was the office of teacher. Chuck Smith and the Calvary Chapel movement played a large part in the Jesus People movement that emerged in 1967. Smith and other ministers, like Jack Hayford, systematically went through the Bible as they taught their churches from the Word of God. In the late 60s and early 1970s, teachers were also emerging from the Word of Faith movement, like Kenneth Hagin and Kenneth Copeland. Other prominent teachers during this time included Derek Prince, Don Basham, Ern Baxter, and Charles Simpson.

In the 1980s, the office of prophet emerged in the wake of "the

Third Wave," described by Peter Wagner as "a gradual opening of straightline evangelical churches to the supernatural ministry of the Holy Spirit."[35] A key component to the Third Wave was John Wimber and the Vineyard church movement. Wimber was the one to introduce the world to the Kansas City prophets: Paul Cain, Bob Jones, John Paul Jackson, Mike Bickle, Jill Austin, and James Goll. A diverse array of significant prophetic voices arose in the 80s, including Rick Joyner, Cindy Jacobs, Chuck Pierce, and Lou Engle, who has been and still is a prophet in my life.

Then in the 1990s, with the outpourings in Toronto and Brownsville, the office of apostle was starting to be recognized—the modern-day apostle. This includes the emergence of apostolic networks and what Peter Wagner called "Microsoft apostles."

A New Wineskin for Revival

So, where does that leave us now? As Bill Hamon's book so accurately proclaims, we are in "the day of the saints." We are in a time where we are witnessing the move of the Holy Spirit equipping the saints—all of God's people—to be ministers. Only a small percentage of the Body of Christ is called to full-time ministry, but I believe that every follower of Jesus is called to be a minister of the gospel, an ambassador for Christ who will transform the world.

What we are seeing today is the progressive restoration of apostles and prophets for the Body of Christ to move forward with this fresh move of God. A lot of people may say this teaching is only confined to a small sect of Christians who are willing to embrace the apostolic and prophetic ministries. On the contrary, I believe what Peter Wagner called a new "apostolic reformation" is taking place.

In his book *Apostles Today*, Peter presented the convincing argument that we are in the second apostolic age, and he described this reformation as a fresh implementation of biblically based church government. This is not about denominational titles but rather functional roles in the Church. The apostolic reformation we are talking about is characterized by modern-day apostles who are leading networks and bringing about reformation. Peter taught that the restoration of apostles is going to bring as much transformative change both to the Church and to society as the Protestant Reformation.[36] I wholeheartedly believe that, because I have seen the fruit. (If you want to learn more about how the apostolic is meant to operate in the Body of Christ today, check out my book *Modern-Day Apostles*.)

I am convinced that the end-time revival we have been contending for will surpass all previous moves of God in church history. The Body of Christ today needs to embrace the structure that God has set forth for us to navigate and oversee such a mighty revival. With all offices of the fivefold ministry in full operation, nothing will be able to hold back the Church from experiencing radical new levels of God's glory on the earth.

Chapter 3

REVIVAL SPREADS THROUGH APOSTOLIC NETWORKS

★ ★ ★ ★ ★

We are living in exciting times, and apostles today are serving as the catalysts for the heightened global advancement of God's Kingdom.

I realize not everyone would agree with me, but I am thoroughly convinced that apostles are meant to play a critical role in the modern Church. God not only gave His people the gifts of the fivefold ministry, which include apostles, but He also gave the apostles an assignment —to disciple nations. As a central key to fulfilling the Great Commission, apostles must equip the Body of Christ for the work of ministry (see Ephesians 4:11-12). This speaks of aligning believers to be effective ministers of the Kingdom.

I like to say that apostles are first revivalists. They preach the gospel of the Kingdom, heal the sick, cast out demons, and advance the Kingdom of God. As delineated in my book *Modern-Day Apostles*, my working definition of an apostle is "a Christlike ambassador with extraordinary authority called and sent out by Jesus Christ with a specific assignment to align the Church to bring Heaven's culture to earth and fulfill the mandate to disciple nations."[37]

A great example of an apostolic revivalist is my good friend Bill Johnson, who pastors Bethel Church in Redding, California. Over the years, Bill has fostered a church culture where signs, wonders, and healings are the norm. Today, Redding is one of the key revival hotspots in the United States. I have seen for myself that there is such a spirit of revival in Redding, as souls are coming to Christ, people are being healed, and the city is being transformed.

Revival is spreading around the world through apostles, and a key to that expansion is specifically through apostolic networks. In church history and especially today, apostolic networks act as catalysts for revival.

Dr. C. Peter Wagner, an internationally respected leader in church growth, recorded, "Church growth analysts are beginning to identify apostolic networks as a modern movement. World-changing leaders and movements are arising to establish progressive structures for families of churches and ministries."[38] Even in the cases when leaders may not call them "apostolic networks," we can identify the same principle or dynamic at work.

Changing Culture Through the Apostolic

Randall Collins, a retired sociologist who is a professor at the University of Pennsylvania, concluded in his seminal work *The Sociology of Philosophies* that three things are necessary to change culture. While he is not known as an Evangelical believer, Collins nevertheless captures a truth from Scripture in his explanation of how society is transformed.

First, he affirms that it takes leadership to transform society.[39] In my interpretation, I would say that it takes *apostles*. As the Body of Christ, we are meant to be an apostolic people. Not everyone in the Church is a prophet or an evangelist, yet we are called to be a prophetic people and to evangelize. The same is true of our apostolic call.

The term "apostle," *apostolos* in Koine Greek, was used by the Romans during the time of Caesar Augustus. Caesar knew that to transform the conquered territories in the Roman Empire, he would have to send out representatives to bring Roman law and order and the Roman culture to those lands. These "sent-out ones" were called apostles. Jesus said that He also has a Kingdom, and He also wants to disciple nations. He is calling His people to bring Kingdom culture to all nations. Therefore, apostles are transformers.

Secondly, to enact social transformation, Collins says that you must go to the *cultural centers* of a given nation.[40] In the United States, our cultural centers would be New York City, Washington, D.C., and Los Angeles. As far as Christian cultural centers in America, you may think of Colorado Springs; Wheaton, Illinois; Redding, California; Birmingham, Alabama; and Harrisburg, Pennsylvania.

You may be asking yourself, "Why are we, as the Body of Christ, not transforming the United States?" The answer is that we are not active enough in our country's cultural centers. That is why with our network Harvest International Ministry (HIM), we have made it a goal to plant an apostolic center in every world-class city, because that is how transformation is going to be sparked. Thank God we are in cities like New York, San Francisco, London, Amsterdam, Seoul, Tokyo, and Osaka, Japan, as we are making some progress. But we need to concert our efforts globally and continue to expand into more world-class cultural centers.

Thirdly, Collins says you cannot change culture individually; it must be done through a *network of people*.[41] This observation is brilliant. When HIM was birthed in 1996, God highlighted to me specific ways that Scripture supports the idea of networking to advance the Kingdom. The New Testament sets the precedent for an apostolic church model that existed in the first century Antioch. In Acts 13, Paul and Barnabas were sent forth from the Antioch church as their first apostolic team. They were on a mission to share the gospel and plant churches in unreached areas of the known world at the time. The church at Antioch was made up of multiethnic and prophetic leaders who were committed to prayer, worship, and missions.

The Exponential Potential of Networks

Networks (apostolic or otherwise) have immense potential to mold and reshape society, for good or bad.

There is a stunning book called *After the Ball*, written by the neuropsychologist Marshall Kirk and Hunter Madsen in 1989. It is about a historic meeting in February 1988 in Warrenton, Virginia, where 175 top gay activists met for a weekend retreat. They decided to come together for a "War Conference" to strategize how to change people's perception of the gay community, with the ultimate goal being to legalize same-sex marriage.[42] The network of activists assembled what was in essence a huge marketing plan. In their strategy they wrote:

> "To make our movement what it should be, and to advance our cause in this society...First, we recommend a nation-wide media campaign to promote a positive image of gays and lesbians. Every

organization—national, state, and local—must accept the responsibility. We must consider the media in every project we undertake… Our media efforts are fundamental to the full acceptance of us in American life."[43]

In formulating their 30-year plan, they covered all their bases, including the decision to change the terminology. Instead of calling themselves "homosexuals," they deliberated to use the word "gay" because they wanted to give the impression that they are happy people. They also skillfully twisted the terminology that it is sexual discrimination if you oppose their agenda, making it an issue of civil rights. Prior to this meeting, it was never a civil rights issue. But now they made it equal, calling it "gay rights." So, if you are against what gays believe, you are labeled as bigoted or intolerant.[44]

Thus, the concerted efforts of this network completely changed the narrative in the United States regarding homosexuality. And sure enough, they were ahead of schedule. In 2015, the U.S. Supreme Court ruled in *Obergefell v. Hodges* to legalize same-sex marriage in all 50 states. This is an example of how "the sons of this age are more shrewd in relation to their own kind than the sons of light" (Luke 16:8). If unbelievers can catalyze remarkable societal change like this, how much more should we as Christians?

The Moravians of Herrnhut

Throughout church history we can find many apostolic networks that helped spread revival in their generation. The Moravians of Herrnhut are a shining example of what one apostolic network can do.

Nikolaus Ludwig von Zinzendorf (1700-1760) was an Austrian nobleman who encountered God at the tender age of four and started to recognize his divine calling early in his life. When he received a considerable inheritance in 1722, Count Zinzendorf felt the conviction to use his wealth and zeal for God to establish a Christ-centered community in Saxony (modern-day Germány). Within a few months, a small band of Protestant believers had found refuge on Zinzendorf's estate after fleeing persecution from the Catholic state in Moravia. Other Moravian and Bohemian families would soon follow, and the new community of religious refugees was called Herrnhut, "The Lord's Watch."

By 1726, Herrnhut had expanded to 300 members belonging to a variety of faith backgrounds, including Anabaptists, Separatists, Calvinists, and even Catholics. With diversity, however, came division, misunderstandings, and sometimes sharp disagreements. Count Zinzendorf honestly assessed the situation and led the community into a season of reconciliation where they committed themselves to live in unity and brotherly love. In August 1727, the Spirit of God started to move powerfully among the Herrnhut believers, who were gathering together to seek the Lord in one accord. As a result, they resolved to begin 24/7 prayer, with one man and one woman pledging to "unceasing prayer" for each hour of the day.

Roberts Liardon records, "Before long, they had seventy-seven people committed to take part in twenty-four-hour prayer, and they received two thousand prayer requests from Christians throughout Saxony... Imagine the astonishment of those prayer warriors had they known that their prayer meeting, under the anointing of the Holy Spirit, would continue among the Moravian Brethren twenty -four hours a day, every day, 365 days a year—*for the next one hundred years!*"[45]

The following year—as Herrnhut continued to grow and daily intercession went on unhindered—Zinzendorf created "bands," or small groups, where each individual could foster his or her faith among other like members of the community. These groups grew in size (later called "choirs"), as did the members' devotion to God. Their passion for Jesus would lay "the foundation for the true call of Zinzendorf and the Moravian Church—launching Protestant missionaries from Europe to the farthest corners of the world."[46]

In 1732, the Moravians sent out their first two missionaries to preach the gospel in the West Indies. Thus, a movement was birthed that would take over 70 missionaries—out of a community of less than 600 people—to the nations over the next 20 years. Fulfilling his apostolic calling, Count Zinzendorf commissioned and financed the mission network that was beginning to spread revival. The Moravians brought the power of Christ to Greenland and Georgia, Surinam and South Africa, Algeria and Amsterdam, Ceylon, Constantinople, North America, and so on. Some people in the community even sold themselves into slavery to reach the slaves with the Good News. During this time, as the prayers of the Moravians continued to faithfully ascend, the First Great Awakening broke out in 1738.

By 1760, some 226 Moravian missionaries had answered the call to help fulfill the Great Commission. By 1782, they had baptized over 11,000 new believers across the globe. "On the Caribbean island of Antigua alone, from 1769 to 1792, the number of converts grew from 14 to 7,400!"[47] The legacy left by Count Zinzendorf and the Moravian Church is truly incredible.

The Clapham Network of England

Another network that enacted radical, lasting change was the Clapham Group. At the turn of the 19th century, English parlia-mentarian William Wilberforce was part of a prominent group of Evangelical Christians who were passionate about ending slavery and responding to various other social issues of the day. The Clapham Group, also called the Clapham Circle or Clapham Sect, was based in the London suburb of Clapham where an informal community of friends soon became a tight-knit team of activists and influencers.

While Wilberforce was a central figure in the group, the Clapham Circle involved a diverse lineup, including Henry Thornton, John Venn, James Stephen, Granville Sharp, Zachary Macaulay, Hannah More, and others. This small but mighty group was made up of Parliament members, pastors, business leaders, lawyers, writers, and more. As we will see in greater detail in Chapter 7, the Clapham Group was instrumental in helping Wilberforce transform England by abolishing slavery. And it could not have been done without the existence of an apostolic network.

In the mind of Henry Thornton, the man who first thought up the Clapham Circle, the creation of a community surrounding Wilberforce had two primary benefits: (1) to strengthen each member's faith and (2) to provide mutual support strategically, relationally, and practically in the group's bold endeavors, abolition being the foremost. "Such communities," says Eric Metaxas, "have often been at the core of movements."[48]

Clapham's scope was both immediate and far reaching. Personal devotion to God—a vital part of life for many members in the Clapham network—sparked a variety of campaigns that left no corner of society unreached. The upper and lower classes were not only the targets but the beneficiaries of Clapham's endeavors, touching on social, political, and moral subjects. This dynamic network used each member's unique skillsets to create a movement—disseminating petitions, conducting thorough research, organizing boycotts, and writing pamphlets, poems, and treatises.[49] They effectively used a multitude of creative outlets to advocate their cause, and thus reeducate the English population about the true nature of slavery.

In her book *Fierce Convictions*, Karen Swallow Prior describes the activities of the Clapham network in this way:

"As a whole, the Clapham community functioned as a large, extended family, rather like the body as described in the New Testament… Although they operated as one body, the genius of the group lay in capitalizing on the particular gifts of each member. They assigned tasks based on each person's gifts and skills in order to accomplish their common causes." [50]

For over 40 years, Clapham fought the good fight and endeavored to rid the British Empire of slavery. The apostolic nature of this network—founded to reform and transform society—superseded all class and political barriers as Christians from various faith backgrounds, and even unbelievers, joined forces to shape history. Clapham was marked by extraordinary unity among its members, and their consistent support of one another would prove to be necessary in their decades-long struggle to abolish slavery.[51]

Rooted in their faith and service to God, the group's reformation campaign ultimately proved effective for both national reform and international impact. Thanks to Clapham's network, slavery ended in the British Empire without a single gunshot. Thus, the long-term effects of revival were spread in a powerful way to see society transformed in England.

Nigeria's Redeemed Christian Church of God

In today's world, the greatest move of the Holy Spirit is likewise taking place among apostles. In Africa, revival is happening in many places, including Mozambique and Kenya. But if there is a revival epicenter in Africa, Nigeria is it. The move of God in Nigeria has had a particular connection to the Redeemed Christian Church of God (RCCG), an apostolic network based in Lagos.

The RCCG has an amazing church-planting philosophy. After they plant a church, they watch to see if it starts to become too large. When it does, they split to create more branches of the church. Consequently, the RCCG is one of the world's fastest-growing churches. In Nigeria alone, they have over 14,000 branches.

What is remarkable about the Redeemed Church is that they have not only evangelized their own nation, but they have also taken Jesus' mandate seriously to take the gospel to the ends of the earth. As of 2017, the RCCG has planted churches in nearly 200 nations. They have even sent missionaries to America, where they have planted over 2,000 churches. Praise God!

Enoch Adeboye, the apostle and general overseer of the RCCG network, has been a willing vessel to advance God's Kingdom in Nigeria. When the Redeemed Church gathers all their people together from around the world, they have 5 million people under one roof! Can you imagine a conference like that? This is made possible because they created a covered pavilion the size of 87 football fields.[52] Besides conferences, the RCCG convenes a monthly prayer meeting with half a million participants. The Holy Spirit's work through this apostolic network has truly been astounding.

The Chinese House Church Movement

With a population of 1.4 billion people, a rapidly expanding economy, and a role as a major exporter of global goods, China also has one of the fastest-growing churches in the world. Indeed, China is on track to become the home to more Christians than any other nation by the year 2030. This makes sense when you see how the number of Chinese Christians has skyrocketed during the past 40 years. Every year since 1979, there has been, on average, a 10% increase of the number of Protestants in China.[53]

Most of the Christians in China are part of the "underground" house church movement, which stands in stark contrast with the government-sanctioned churches under the umbrella of the China Christian Council, Catholic Patriotic Association, and Three-Self Patriotic Movement. Nevertheless, inside the Chinese governing political party, one in every five members is now a born-again believer. David Aikman, in his book *Jesus in Beijing*, writes, "It is significant that Christianity is emerging in China at a time when there is a massive ideological vacuum left in society by the nation-wide collapse of belief in Marxism-Leninism."[54]

I have traveled to China many times and have personally seen the wide-reaching extent of the underground churches. God called me to China over 40 years ago in a vision, so I have carried this country on my heart for most of my life. It has been amazing to see the transformation and rapid growth of the church and to see leaders rise to empower the next generation, even in the midst of persecution.

To give just one example, I am blown away by Brother Xi (not his real name but a pseudonym), who leads one of five underground house church movements in mainland China. All five are led by an apostle, and the Church in China is growing because of them. The leaders, however, are not called apostles; they are called "uncles." I had the honor of meeting all five leaders around 10 years ago in a meeting set up by Peter Wagner.

The numbers in the House Church movement are staggering. Brother Xi comes from a city of 10 million people. Out of those 10 million, half are born again! And then out of those 5 million believers, 2.5 million are part of Brother Xi's apostolic network. Brother Xi has also planted a church in every city with a population of 10 million or more in China. Given the nation's immense population, there are currently at least 16 cities with more than 10 million inhabitants.

In addition to churches, Brother Xi is now planting businesses throughout Muslim nations along the Silk Road, including Afghanistan, Iraq, Iran, and Pakistan. He knows that his Chinese passport is an entryway to the Middle East, and he is determined to use it to help bring in the harvest. He may not be able to openly plant churches in these countries, but he has taken up the brilliant strategy of planting businesses.

Because of their status as Chinese businessmen, Brother Xi and his colleagues are welcomed into Muslim nations because these nations want the Chinese to invest in them. What these governments don't realize is that these Chinese are Christians, intentionally coming as ambassadors of the Kingdom of God! David Aikman asserts, "There are Christian entrepreneurs at every level of Chinese society, including some of the richest men in the country."[55] Thus, the Chinese can do things in Muslim nations that Westerners, such as those with a U.S. or Canadian passport, cannot do. With each business started, an underground church is planted to reach the Muslims with the Gospel of Jesus Christ.

It is amazing to note that large numbers of the Chinese House Church believers have a strong determination to bring the gospel to the Muslim world. This is something that has been generally lacking in most churchgoers in the West. The apostolic network of China's Christians has responded proactively to this divine call that is part of advancing God's Kingdom and spreading revival in the 10/40 window.[56]

New Apostolic Church Movements

The move of God that is emerging around the world is advancing in large part thanks to apostolic networks. A variety of apostolic networks were birthed in the 1990s: Partners in Harvest led by John Arnott, Iris Ministries led by Heidi and Rolland Baker, Global Awakening led by Randy Clark, Global Legacy led by Bill Johnson, and Harvest International Ministry, which I founded in 1996. Additionally, Calvary Chapel and the Vineyard movement, while they may not use this term, were birthed and led by apostolic leaders, Chuck Smith and John Wimber, respectively.

As we have seen, revival is exploding in Africa, mainly through independent churches and apostolic networks, like the RCCG. Iris Ministries is another reason for this powerful expansion of God's Kingdom. Originating in 1995, Iris is based in Pemba, Mozambique, and has launched ministries throughout various regions of Africa, Asia, the Middle East, Latin America, and North America. In their ministry to unreached villages in Mozambique, the gospel is always preached with signs and wonders following.

The deaf hear, the blind see, and the poor have good news preached to them. When Heidi gives an invitation to receive Christ, her team follows up and plants a new church right there on the spot. They organize a church service the following day, and thus a new church is built from the ground up. Iris Ministries has planted over 10,000 churches following this pattern.[57] From what I have personally witnessed, Iris is one of the most amazing church-planting movements in the world.

With all our endeavors at HIM, God made it clear to us that we were to invite other churches to partner with us as we work to advance His Kingdom in both unreached and frequently reached nations. We came to the realization that on our own we can only accomplish so much. But by networking with thousands of other churches who are aligned with our vision, our Kingdom-hearted synergy would create serious damage in the enemy's camp. Thus we became a network of networks. The Great Commission isn't an undertaking for "lone wolf" evangelists. It is a collective, communal, and apostolic call for the entire Body of Christ to be actively engaged in. We emphasize the apostolic nature of our ministry because we recognize the value that Scripture places on the apostolic. We do not only want to participate in what God is doing today around the world; we want to be part of the way God is doing it.

We know full well that we are only one of many apostolic networks that God has been raising up as fresh wineskins for a global harvest. We are simply delighted to be part of bringing in the harvest! Yet the continued response of like-hearted and sincere world-changers continues to amaze me. I consider it a privilege to serve with the most incredible group of loving, Spirit-led history makers the world has ever known!

Chapter 4

REVIVAL SUCCESS CAN LEAD TO TERRIBLE FAILURE

★ ★ ★ ★ ★

When I was working toward my M.Div. at Fuller Seminary in the 1980s, I was privileged to study under gifted Charismatic professors like C. Peter Wagner, Charles Kraft, and Bobby Clinton. Apart from the mandatory courses in my program, I deliberately took all my electives in the School of World Mission where these incredible theologians taught.

While at Fuller, we learned about a principle known as "redemption and lift." According to this principle, wherever the gospel goes throughout the world and is received, it lifts people out of poverty. But here is the catch: Revival is a two-edged sword. On one hand, revival does bring prosperity and blessing in its wake. On the other hand, prosperity—when it is not handled correctly—will corrupt the church and cause the church to decline. This is something that we vigilantly need to guard ourselves from.

We can see that wherever revival has broken out in church history, it has brought material prosperity and blessing in its wake. In his study of revival, Winkie Pratney, one of my mentors, affirms the same pattern that each outpouring of the Spirit "was followed by a period of national prosperity."[58] Yet by the same token, increased material blessings can lead to the routinization of the church. You can have all the money and all the blessing that God's redemptive gift brings, but without the presence of God, you have nothing. That is why we must stay hungry for the things of God.

Walking the Divine Tightrope

There is a divine tension that should mark our walk as believers: God wants us to be hungry *and* full at the same time. You and I are to be continually full of the Holy Spirit, yet we are to be continually hungry for more of Him. That is the real challenge for believers, when revival comes, to stay humble and hungry.

In the Sermon on the Mount, Jesus instructs us: "Blessed are the poor in spirit, for theirs is the kingdom of heaven. Blessed are those who mourn, for they will be comforted. Blessed are the gentle, for they will inherit the earth. Blessed are those who hunger and thirst for righteousness, for they will be satisfied" (Matthew 5:3-6). In Matthew 5:5, the word "gentle" can also be translated as "humble." This section of the Beatitudes shows us the vital importance of cultivating hungry and thirsty hearts for the Lord. This, in turn, will help us to stay free from the love of money.

The Dangers of Materialism

Korea is a classic example of redemption and lift. In the 1950s and

1960s, South Korea was one of the poorest nations on earth. In 1961, the nation's GDP per capita was less than $100.[59] This was a byproduct of the devastating effects of the Korean War (1950-1953), World War II (1939-1945), and the Japanese occupation (1905-1945).

Today, South Korea has the 10th largest economy in the world,[60] with a GDP per capita of over $31,000. In such a short span of time, there was a dramatic shift economically. Many popular products with a global distribution are made in South Korea, including Samsung and Hyundai. Korea has excelled not only economically but also in terms of cultural capital; K-pop and Korean soap operas wield tremendous influence over a large fanbase located across the world.

To set the backdrop for this incredible tale of prosperity, the Church in Korea exploded because of the foundation of the Pyong-yang Revival that broke out in 1907. That proved to be the impetus for some of the world's largest churches. (Read more about this revival in Chapter 5.)

When I first started going to Korea with our network HIM, the Church was growing rapidly, with Dr. David Yonggi Cho's Full Gospel Church figuring most prominently among churches in Seoul. One of the reasons I initially didn't want to go to Korea was because I thought, "Do they really need us? We need them!" In my mind, I thought we should be planting churches among unreached people groups, but Korea already had so many large churches in existence. It is stunning when you are in Seoul at night because every church building has a red cross lit up and you see red crosses just about everywhere.

For quite some time, the Church in Korea was experiencing significant growth. Peter Wagner, who was on Yonggi Cho's board for a number of years, accompanied me on many of those trips, as he was studying the growth of the church in Korea. According to Peter, the number of evangelicals in Korea should have easily hit 25% or 30%, but it ended up plateauing at 18% and then started to decline.

There are different factors that have influenced that stagnation in the Korean church. One factor is age, as the revival generation of my grandparents' time didn't reach the younger generation, and many of them have now passed away. Another reason is that the nation prospered financially in the wake of the move of God, but they didn't know how to handle the prosperity. They also didn't know that a spirit of Mammon was released. I believe behind this is the sin of the love of money (see 1 Timothy 6:10). Sadly, the Church in Korea started to decline as the nation as a whole prospered.

The number of Christians in Korea today has dropped down to 16% because materialism and the spirit of Mammon have been really choking the Church in that nation. Globalization and modernity have taken a toll on the spiritual climate. Generally speaking, the younger generation of Koreans today are very secular and materialistic. As one example of globalization, pornography that was produced in Los Angeles can easily make its way to Korea and has really choked the life of the Church there.

One clear outward sign of this spiritual stagnation is what most Koreans choose to do on their sabbath day. As their spiritual fervor lessened, they started investing their time playing golf on Sundays. (You may have noticed that many of the best women golfers in the world are Korean.) While they used to go to church on Sundays, they are now rationalizing their decision to use their sabbath to play golf instead, as they work the other six days of the week. These are the same people who would go to early morning prayer meetings six days a week. In years past, every church used to have an early morning prayer meeting. If you were a pastor in Korea, you had to lead prayer at your church before the workday began.

That is precisely why, back in the early days of Harvest Rock

Church, Lou Engle told me I had to be at our early morning prayer meetings—because I am a Korean pastor! I responded, "Look, Lou. I may be Korean, but I'm actually a banana: yellow on the outside and white inside" (I may be ethnically Korean, but I'm culturally not Korean). He said, "It doesn't matter. You have to lead by example, and we're praying." And that is how he would drag me out of bed every morning to pray! (By the way, we still have early morning prayer meetings at 6 a.m., six days a week at Harvest Rock Church.)

Unfortunately, in Korea today you no longer see many pastors holding early morning prayer meetings. They also used to have all-night prayer meetings every Friday night. It was just part of their church culture. Sadly, there was a decline in the church because they got so comfortable with the prosperity.

Please hear my heart in this. I recognize that the churches in Korea are using their finances to advance the Kingdom of God. In fact, Korea is the number-one mission-giving nation *per capita*, even more than the United States. Korea is on God's heart, and I believe a fresh wave of revival will sweep across this nation once again.

A Common Stumbling Block

So many nations that have experienced a move of the Holy Spirit have been similarly wounded by the double-edged blade of prosperity. Brazil is dealing with this issue. What happens is that many churches in Brazil were very poor before experiencing revival. When the harvest comes in and they become megachurches, they are now flushed with cash, which the leadership is unprepared to steward wisely. So, we are now witnessing that money has corrupted pastors. (I share more about this problem—and God's solution—in Chapter 11.)

This is taking place in China as well. As I am sure you are aware, China is growing economically with staggering numbers. China ranks second in GDP behind the United States, and it will soon be number one.

The revival that broke out in China was a rural revival. It took place primarily in the countryside. However, the rural believers are moving to major cities, like Beijing, Shanghai, and Guangzhou, to get jobs. One of two things is happening as a result. Some are bringing the revival with them to the city—praise God! But many of them are prospering so much that they are leaving the church. They've lost their hunger and spiritual edge that they once had in the more rural areas of mainland China.

The same thing also happened in Europe. As they prospered, they lost their spiritual edge. Instead of using money to advance God's Kingdom, they gave in to the world of material comforts. This is what Revelation 2:4 means when it says, "You have left your first love," as sins of pride can manifest.

Pride Goes Before the Fall

The other issue is that pastors and leaders can become overnight celebrities. For some, the attention goes to their head. Others meanwhile become jealous of their position, wealth, or fame. Both responses, selfish ambition and jealousy, cause real demise in the church. James 3:14-16 gives us a clear warning:

> "But if you have bitter jealousy and selfish ambition in your heart, do not be arrogant and so lie against the truth. This wisdom is not that which comes down from above, but is earthly, natural, demonic. For where jealousy and selfish ambition exist, there is disorder and every evil thing."

God has lovingly rebuked me to make sure that I guard my heart from selfish ambition. My goal is to make Jesus' name famous and not my own. He deserves all the praise and glory. *"Not to us, O LORD, not to us, but to your name* give glory, for the sake of *your* steadfast love and *your* faithfulness!"* (Psalm 115:1, ESV).

During my lifetime in America, the Charismatic movement birthed great ministries like *The 700 Club* and TBN, but there were also unfortunate scandals in other ministries like PTL with televangelist Jim Bakker. In his book entitled *I Was Wrong*, Bakker candidly shares about his mistakes and repents of his failures relating to lust, power, and money. He spent five years in prison not because of committing the egregious sin of adultery, but because he defrauded people of their timeshares in his Heritage Village by selling more than he had available to lease out. It was specifically tied to greed.

Jim Bakker emerged from jail a changed man, and one of the first places he spoke at was Harvest Rock Church. I remember him saying, "Every person that was in prison, I could trace it to the love of money." The Word of God describes this plainly in 1 Timothy 6:10: "For the love of money is a root of all sorts of evil, and some by longing for it have wandered away from the faith and pierced themselves with many griefs." Indeed, the love of money is a huge snare. But through accountability, discipline, and the power of the Holy Spirit, we can stay clear of its pitfalls.

Prosperity with a Purpose

We can see how globalization, modernization, and materialism have really stifled the church. We need to learn from that and guard ourselves from the enemy's tactics. Prosperity and modernity are a double-edged sword that can bless a nation or cause the church to decline.

A few years ago, Bill Johnson personally told me that his greatest fear is the success of the Bethel movement, because he knows church history. When you are successful, you can start getting lax, compromising, becoming proud because of your prosperity. We must remember that the blessing of God is meant to be used to advance the Kingdom.

I'll never forget when I heard Robert Morris, the Senior Pastor of Gateway Church based in Dallas, talk about the life of Joseph. As the book of Genesis recounts, Joseph passed the *purity* test when Potiphar's wife tried to seduce him. Then he went through the prison test as he persevered for several years in the king's prison. But the biggest danger was when he became the second most powerful person in Egypt, and he faced the *prosperity* test. That is when the temptations are the greatest. We have to learn this lesson from church history—revival's success can lead to the decline and failure of the church if we are not careful and vigilant.

Probably nothing reveals character as quickly as how we handle money. Jesus made it clear that God will not entrust us with His greater spiritual possessions if we cannot be trusted with material possessions first (see Luke 16:10-11). God uses prosperity to cultivate our self-control and to help clarify our spiritual maturity. After all, God is primarily interested in our heart attitude when we give, not the size of our wallet. He is far more concerned with the quality of the giver than the quantity of the gift.

When God knows that He can get prosperity *through* us, He will send it *to* us. God wants to bless His people so much that we are a blessing to the nations of the earth. He wants us to prosper. But let me clarify something: This idea is not to be confused with the "prosperity gospel." At Harvest Rock Church, we believe in prosperity with a purpose. We don't preach that God wants to bless you just so you are prosperous, as an end unto itself. We present the biblical teaching that God wants to "supply all your needs according to His riches in glory in Christ Jesus" (Philippians 4:19). In Genesis

12:2-3, the Lord tells Abraham, "I will bless you, and make your name great; and so you shall be a blessing... And in you all the families of the earth will be blessed." The same applies to us today. We are blessed so we can be a blessing to others.

It is so important to understand this truth. We as Christians are so committed to the Great Commission. But do you realize that it takes money to fulfill the Great Commission? God wants you to be so blessed that not only are all your needs met, but with your surplus you are able to sow into the advancement of God's Kingdom.

Our focus should always be on the gospel of the Kingdom, not on prosperity by itself. The prosperity that God blesses us with is always meant to be used to bring in the harvest. Think of how many missionaries you could fund, how many orphans you could clothe, and how many unreached people groups you could evangelize with an overflow of prosperity in your life!

The Transfer of Wealth: A Paradigm Shift

In Isaiah 60, verses 3 and 5, we find a stunning promise from God: "Nations will come to your light, and kings to the brightness of your rising... Then you will see and be radiant, and your heart will thrill and rejoice; because the abundance of the sea will be turned to you, *the wealth of the nations will come to you.*" Isn't it interesting that Isaiah first talks about nations coming to the light (verse 3), and then suddenly, he says the wealth of the nations will come to you (verse 5)?

The statement in Isaiah 60:5 isn't an isolated verse. Verse 11 of the same chapter says, "Your gates will be open continually; they will not be closed day or night, so that men may bring to you the wealth of the nations, with their kings led in procession." God wants to bless you so much that even while you are sleeping, you are going to prosper. I like the sound of that! This does not mean being a workaholic and running around frantically trying to make more money. I believe the Scripture is talking about a passive or portfolio wealth, like investing in mutual funds or the stock market. Another example is buying a rental property. You are not working harder, but God blesses your investments. Out of a position of rest, you are going to receive prosperity. God is going to give His people knowledge, wisdom, and grace to prosper in the last days so that we can give to the fulfillment of the Great Commission.

I also love what it says in Haggai 2:7-9: "'I will shake all the nations; and *they will come with the wealth of all nations*, and I will fill this house with glory,' says the Lord of hosts. *'The silver is Mine and the gold is Mine,'* declares the Lord of hosts. 'The latter glory of this house will be greater than the former… and in this place I will give peace'…."

In both of these passages in Isaiah and Haggai, we find that the arrival of the Lord's "greater" glory coincides with a great transfer of wealth. This makes sense when you look at the context for the passage in Haggai, which is primarily dealing with finances. Haggai was trying to raise money to rebuild the Temple under Zerubbabel. It is an offering letter, if you will.

In Haggai 2:8, God says, "The silver is Mine and the gold is Mine." One of the greatest truths that the Lord has taught us is that everything is God's, and we are just stewards of what we have been given. Psalm 24:1 (NKJV) says, "The earth is the Lord's, and all its fullness, the world and those who dwell therein." God has called us to be good stewards of everything in life.

My wife and I have cultivated a mentality of stewardship, so that every cent that God gives us, we are going to use well. That translates to doing simple things like eating leftovers (the average American throws away 40% of their food), recycling, turning off the lights and air when we leave hotels, and picking up trash off the ground. We are not legalistic about it, but we know that we will one day stand before the judgment seat of Jesus and will be rewarded based on how we stewarded our time, money, relationships, and basically our whole life (see 2 Corinthians 5:10). As a result, God has blessed us with even more of His abundance. For example, if you are faithful with money, God will give you true riches (see Luke 16:11).

We are meant to *live to give*. It is our goal to develop a culture of generosity in our church and ministries. This doesn't just mean being faithful with our tithes and offerings. It starts there, but it will naturally expand to increased generosity. "The generous man will be prosperous, and he who waters will himself be watered" (Proverbs 11:25). Give to those who are in need in your community. Treat your friends from church to lunch. Sow extravagantly into ministries that are advancing God's Kingdom. There is no limit to how much you can give. Honestly, our goal is to give away 90% of all our income. I believe that this is the primary way that God can break the spirit of Mammon as you continue to prosper. After all, you cannot out-give God!

God wants you to use your finances to win your family members. When they see the extraordinary blessing and prosperity in your life, they will ask what is different about you and they will be attracted to the divine favor that is on you. That may translate into the blessings in your marriage, the way you parent your children, the favor at your job, the prosperity in your finances, and every area of your life.

I believe that God is going to release financial breakthrough to His people because He wants to bring a historic harvest of souls into His Kingdom. The seeds you sow into the harvest fields will be multiplied to change lives, transform cities, and disciple nations. God wants to bless you with radical blessings—and with the Christlike character to steward them well!

PART 2:

CHARACTERISTICS OF HISTORIC REVIVAL

★ ★ ★ ★ ★

WHAT DOES REVIVAL LOOK LIKE?

★ ★ ★ ★ ★

You may have heard Christians talk about a "renewal," an "outpouring," or an "awakening" when referring to a move of God. But when we talk about revival, we have to be in agreement with our terminology because revival means so many different things to different people.

For example, my dad, a Charismatic Southern Baptist pastor (who went to be with the Lord in 2010), would periodically hold "revival services." What did "revival" look like in his context? My dad would bring in a guest speaker from South Korea or another Korean church in America, and they would have church meetings scheduled over a certain weekend. Now, those were good evangelistic services, and we should praise God for them and have as many of them as possible. But, objectively speaking, that is not true revival.

I like the way my covenant brother Lou Engle described revival years ago: "Revival is *God's* arrival." It is when Jesus comes and manifests Himself and His Kingdom on earth as it is in heaven. Revival is heaven invading earth. It is Acts 2, when the followers of Jesus were together in one accord and suddenly a sound came from heaven. It didn't come from them. Then crowds gathered together to hear the sound that had come down from heaven, and then they heard the 120 believers speaking in tongues. This is heaven coming to earth.

Often referred to as The Lord's Prayer, Matthew 6:10 is actually a revival prayer: "Your kingdom come. Your will be done, on earth as it is in heaven." Over the past 2,000 years, the Church has been praying for the Kingdom, the rule of God, to be established and manifested on earth. In essence, we have been praying for Revival with a capital "R."

In Part 2 of this book, I want to focus on three characteristics of historic revival. These characteristics will help us to recognize the tangible results that come when the Spirit of God moves powerfully in any given nation. They will also help to inspire heavenly strategies to see historic revival come to fruition in our own nation.

Chapter 5

THE CHURCH IS REVIVED

★ ★ ★ ★ ★

Since the start of the 2020s, I believe the Church at large has been in a season of returning to God. Repentance is crucial when it comes to revival. Scripture shows a clear pattern that repentance precedes the outpouring of the Holy Spirit (see Joel 2:12-28 and Acts 2:37-38). That definitely rings true in this present season. As all the nations of the earth have been shaken, paradigms have shifted, and the global *Ekklesia* has been coming together to consecrate ourselves afresh to God and renew our commitment to see revival in our homes, cities, and nations.

The first characteristic of historic revival is that the Church is revived by the Spirit of God. Throughout church history, we see that every revival began when an individual or a group of people experienced a fresh consecration to the Lord and were filled with the power of the Holy Spirit. During the outpouring of revival, the

Church receives a massive revelation of God the Father's love. As we will see, this paves the way for the following characteristics of revival.

Return to Your First Love

In the second and third chapters of Revelation, we find seven letters written to seven churches in Asia Minor (modern-day Turkey) with directives from their Resurrected Savior. It is sobering when you realize that all seven of these churches started out in revival, but over time, five of them had gotten stuck in sin that needed to be brought to the light. Two of the interrelated sins that are dealt with in these chapters are the sin of losing their first love and the sin of lukewarmness.

The first message, written to the church in Ephesus, singles out the fact that the Ephesian believers had "left their first love" (Revelation 2:4, NKJV). Another translation puts it this way: "You have abandoned the passionate love you had for me at the beginning" (TPT).

This blows me away, because a great revival began when the apostle Paul visited Ephesus in Acts 19. God was moving so powerfully that Paul decided to stay there for three years (Acts 20:31), whereas in other cities he only stayed for a few weeks (Acts 17:1-2). The Bible says that "all who lived in Asia [Minor] heard the word of the Lord" because of the apostolic center in Ephesus (Acts 19:10). Ephesus was where extraordinary miracles were being done by the apostle Paul (Acts 19:11). There was so much repentance in that city that everyone who practiced magic and witchcraft brought millions of dollars' worth of books and burned them in the city square (Acts 19:19). And then when Paul left, the next person he put in charge was Timothy (1 Timothy 1:3). How would you like to attend a church where the founding pastor was the apostle Paul and the leader who succeeded him was Timothy? That is quite a church! Plus, church historians tell us that John the Beloved went to Ephesus later on along with Mary, the mother of Jesus, because in my opinion, revival was breaking out and God needed an apostle to oversee this great outpouring of the Holy Spirit.

Despite all of that, 40 years after Paul established the church in Ephesus, Revelation 2 expresses a strong exhortation for the Ephesians to repent and remember from where they had fallen (Revelation 2:5). But this rebuke is redemptive. It is a call to come back and be restored to their first love, Jesus Christ. No matter how many times we may fail, God the Father's arms are always open wide to receive His sons and daughters back into close fellowship with Him.

I believe the Lord today is calling the Church to return to our first love. When the Body of Christ enters a season of revival, God the Father's love is revealed to His children in unparalleled fashion. Love becomes our main focus. We come to the realization that we love because God first loved us (see 1 John 4:19). In John 15:9-12, Jesus says, "Just as the Father has loved Me, I also have loved you; remain in My love. If you keep My commandments, you will remain in My love; just as I have kept My Father's commandments and remain in His love… This is My commandment, that you love one another, just as I have loved you." When our hearts are revived by God's passionate, eternal love, we can then maintain that love by abiding in a place of overflow—where we continually receive His love and pour it out to others.

Encountered by Love

When I got saved at the age of 17, God could have revealed Himself to me in any number of ways, but the way He chose to reveal Himself was through His overwhelming love. Here is a little bit of the context for that dramatic, life-changing encounter that I share in my book *God Wants to Bless You*:

> Growing up in the 1970s, I did not follow in the footsteps of my father, who was a minister. Instead, I rebelled and embraced the hippie culture of sex, drugs and rock 'n' roll. This lifestyle had its fun times, but I started to notice a growing emptiness in my soul.
>
> While at a party one weekend, I felt jaded and frustrated because deep inside I knew there had to be more than I was experiencing. I went to a vacant room, and even though I did not believe in God, I found myself crying out to Him to reveal Himself to me. In that moment, I felt an incredible warmth and love envelop my body. Jesus was reaching out to me, and I was overwhelmed by how much He loved me.
>
> I could not stop weeping for three days as waves of God's love crashed over me again and again. I have never been the same since that experience. To this day, I continue to be undone by the Lord's perfect love and seek to share His love with as many people as I can. I have committed my life to this call because there is no greater knowledge that can be shared than the knowledge of His love.[61]

One thing we must realize is that we repent out of love for God—not out of duty or fear, but love. We must refocus our attention on the First Commandment, to love God with all our heart, soul, mind, and strength (Mark 12:30). This focus, in turn, will lead us to love our neighbor as ourselves.

A Church On Fire

In the third chapter of Revelation, God says to the church in Laodicea, "I know your deeds, that you are neither cold nor hot; I wish that you were cold or hot. So because you are lukewarm, and neither hot nor cold, I will spit you out of My mouth" (Revelation 3:15-16).

When a person first comes to Christ, you may think it will be easy to stay on fire for God until the day you die. Many start off strong, but their faith fizzles out later down the road. It's not how you start the race that counts but how you finish. Living by faith is a marathon, not a sprint. That is why Jesus said, "The one who endures to the end will be saved" (Matthew 24:13, ESV). Every day we have choices to make, and our decision to passionately pursue God will have a ripple effect in our lives as we persevere in our faith.

The Lord is looking for those who are willing to be completely "sold out" for Jesus. If you are spiritually cold, there is hope, because you can be saved and set ablaze with the love of God. God wants us to be "hot" Christians—on fire for Jesus Christ! This is the only kind of Christianity that I know. It has been this way since day one. When I first got saved, I made the decision to make Jesus the Lord of my entire life, and in all these years I have never turned back or compromised my faith, all by the grace of God.

It Begins in God's House

Many of us in the Church like to read what it says in Joel 2:28, "It will come about after this that I will pour out My Spirit on all mankind." But what is God referring to when He says "after this"? Verses 12 and 13 of that chapter contain the answer: "'Yet even now,' declares the Lord, 'Return to Me with all your heart, and with fasting, weeping and mourning; and rend your heart and not your garments.'" This passage continues to exhort us to "consecrate a fast," pray corporately, and for the ministers of the Lord to weep in intercession for His people (Joel 2:14-17).

I am firmly convinced that repentance must begin with the house of God, with God's people. 1 Peter 4:17 says, "For it is time for judgment to begin with the household of God; and if it begins with us first, what will be the outcome for those who do not obey the gospel of God?" Everything rises and falls with the Church.

Repentance Turns to Revival

The Pyongyang Revival of 1907, also known as "the Repentance Revival," was sparked by an intensified season of fasting, prayer, and public repentance. In December 1906, there were American missionaries in Pyongyang, Korea, who had heard about the Welsh Revival of 1904 that was catalyzed through a young man named Evan Roberts. The missionaries were so desperate for revival that they decided to fast for the entire month of December—yes, even during Christmas and New Year celebrations. When the Korean pastors heard about it, they joined the Americans in this radical fast.

At the turn of the new year in 1907, they proceeded to meet every night for prayer. During the first week, nothing extraordinary happened. But on the seventh day, one of the elders of the Pyong-yang Presbyterian church stood up in front of everyone at the prayer meeting. He began to weep as he confessed the sin of stealing money from one of his best friends. The moment he got up, humbled himself, and publicly repented for all to hear, the Spirit of God fell in their midst and the revival began.

The Repentance Revival lasted 45 years and would lay the foundation for some of the world's largest churches, including the late Dr. Yonggi Cho's Full Gospel Church of over 700,000 as well as the largest Presbyterian, Baptist, and Methodist churches at one time.

I want to ask you a question: How desperate are you for revival?

Are you willing to humble yourself as you contend for revival?

In a scripture that is familiar to many, 2 Chronicles 7:14 (NKJV), the Lord promises, "If *My* people who are called by My name will humble themselves, and pray and seek My face, and turn from their wicked ways, then I will hear from heaven, and will forgive their sin and heal their land." Notice that God says, "If My people humble themselves and pray…" He doesn't call out the lost in the world. He doesn't name a political party or corrupt officials. He says it starts with His people. God says revival begins with you, my friend.

Greater Holiness

In this momentous season, there are many things that we can repent of as the Body of Christ. It is imperative that we take responsibility for the sin that we have in our own lives, but it is also important to practice identification repentance for our nation. In Daniel 9:1-3, the prophet Daniel entered a season of prayer and repentance when he saw that the 70 years of exile was coming to completion, as prophesied by Jeremiah before him. We see Daniel repenting for the ungodliness of God's people even though he was a righteous man of God (Daniel 9:4-19). The Bible says that followers of Christ are in right standing with God and are holy before the Lord (2 Corinthians 5:21). While we already have a position of righteousness, we have to *practice* righteousness in the way we live our lives.

Unfortunately, the Church at large has not been practicing righteousness. The Body of Christ needs to hear a fresh call to walk in personal holiness: "But like the Holy One who called you, be holy yourselves also in all your behavior; because it is written, 'You shall be holy, for I am holy'" (1 Peter 1:15-16). As part of the sanctifying work of the Holy Spirit, we are on the path of being transformed and becoming more and more like Christ (2 Corinthians 3:18).

If we are going to see revival come to our land, we must lead lives full of the Spirit and marked by purity. A life of radical, Spirit-inspired holiness is necessary to fuel the advancement of God's Kingdom in our day. This is especially true for those in full-time ministry. In the Church at large, I believe that many pastors need to repent of the Laodicean syndrome of lukewarmness as the result of not preaching the whole counsel of God. Many have shut their mouths for fear that people will be offended and leave the church if we preach on the sins of abortion, homosexuality, pornography, and other controversial issues of our time. We as pastors cannot afford to live lukewarm lives—now more than ever.

One telling example that personally convicted me is when Gov. Newsom, during the lockdown, declared the church as nonessential. Abortion clinics were essential. Marijuana dispensaries were essential. Even strip clubs and casinos were essential, but not the church. I realized that we (I am including myself) have had hardly any impact in California. I found myself repenting on behalf of the Church and her leaders for our nonessential lukewarmness.

It begins with a renewed love for Jesus. We must love Him with all our heart, mind, soul, and strength. And we must preach the whole counsel of God. We must speak the truth in love. We must never compromise the truth of God's Word because of popular opinion in our culture. Holiness is non-negotiable.

Greater Power

To go hand-in-hand with greater holiness, I believe the Church also needs to walk in greater power. In Acts 1:8, Jesus said, "But you will receive *power* when the *Holy Spirit* has come upon you; and you shall be My witnesses both in Jerusalem, and in all Judea and Samaria, and even to the remotest part of the earth." It takes power to get the job done. According to Thayer's Greek Lexicon, the Greek word *dunamis* means "strength," "power," and can specifically denote "the power of performing miracles."[62]

Something we need to realize is that God never intended us to fulfill the Great Commission apart from His power. What God is calling us to do cannot be accomplished in our own strength. We need to depend on the power of God if we want to see revival come to our churches. When we ask the Holy Spirit to fill and empower us, He will enable us to courageously preach the Gospel of the Kingdom with signs and wonders following!

In this same verse, the word for "witness" is *martus*, which is where we get the word "martyr" from. You see, when you are full of the Holy Spirit, you are willing to lay down your life as a martyr for Jesus Christ.

One of the times I went to Mozambique to visit my longtime missionary friends Heidi and Rolland Baker, we were on a flatbed truck preaching when people nearby started to throw stones at us. Heidi looked at me and said, "This is normal." As I was ducking stones, I could hardly believe that she experiences this type of thing every day. What happens is that Heidi goes into "the bush" to do open-air preaching, but the Muslims who hear her become irate. However, when Heidi invites them to bring the blind and the deaf to her, she prays for them, the people get healed, and the whole village gets saved. It is amazing to see the work of God in the Bakers' ministry over the years as thousands of lives have been transformed by the power of the Holy Spirit.

This reminds me of a wonderful example of revival coming first to the Church before spreading out and leading to a great harvest. Isaiah 60:1 says, "The glory of the Lord has risen upon *you*." The glory of God is the manifest presence of God. The Hebrew word for glory is *kabod*, meaning "weight." This is God's weighty presence that comes as a manifestation of revival. That is why some people fall under the power of God as God's glory is manifesting in their midst.

It took a powerful encounter during a season of revival to set Heidi and Rolland Baker on the trajectory they have taken in life. Before they went to experience the Toronto Blessing in 1997, the Bakers were worn-out missionaries desperate for a touch from God. At the Toronto Airport Christian Fellowship, the epicenter for the move of God, Heidi got stuck on the floor for seven days straight! The only time she got up in those seven days was when people carried her to the bathroom. During that experience, Heidi asked God for permission to be carried away to her hotel room, but He responded by saying that He was doing a work in her, so she was not to leave the altar. She spent those seven days only drinking water while completely submerged in the weighty, manifest presence of the Almighty.

Before Heidi went to Toronto, she only had won a few souls, planted a few weak churches, and was caring for a handful of orphans. Since then, she has planted 20,000 churches and is feeding over 10,000 children a day. Thank God for the power of the Holy Spirit!

Revived by Times of Refreshing

In my book *Say Goodbye to Powerless Christianity*, I share how I felt like I was "born again" *again* in Toronto. Before I went there, I was so dry spiritually. Yes, I was a believer who spoke in tongues and had been part of the Charismatic Renewal since 1974. But I was so hungry for more. I was saying, "Where is the God of revival?" Thank God for His merciful outpouring of the Holy Spirit that rescued me from such a low point in my life that I would have even quit the ministry.

The first night of my trip to Toronto, the manifest presence of God was so intense that I thought I might die! By the time I got back to my hotel, I could not walk, so I crawled on all fours in an attempt to get to my room. Believe me, I *wanted* to be on my feet. I didn't want to crawl around on the Regal Constellation Hotel ballroom floor just to get to the elevator. But the power of God was all over me, and that's what I had to do! Still on my hands and knees, I went up the elevator, crawled to my room, opened the door, and rolled onto my bed.

In Toronto there was so much power in those days that you couldn't touch a person without them flopping down backwards. If someone puts their finger into an electric socket, the power of the electricity would impact them severely, maybe even kill them. How much more when we're talking about the power of the Almighty God!

During my Toronto encounter, I shook so hard under the power of God unlike anything I had ever experienced. I was also hit by holy laughter to the point that I could not preach. I like to think of myself as being calm and collected most of the time. But during this period, there were several times when I got up to speak at a conference and I could not open my mouth without laughing. I did not want to laugh—I just wanted to preach! But I couldn't get any words out without laughter taking over. So I just gave up and never ended up preaching on those occasions. Over the course of my life, that has never happened to me except during the revival we experienced in the 1990s. The ways that God moved corporately during those years left a lasting impact on my life and dramatically changed the way I see things.

Acts 3:19-21 says, "Repent therefore, and turn back, that your sins may be blotted out, *that times of refreshing may come from the presence of the Lord*, and that he may send the Christ appointed for you, Jesus, whom heaven must receive until the time for restoring all the things about which God spoke by the mouth of his holy prophets long ago." In the Greek, the word "refreshing" (*anapsuxis*) literally means a cooling or recovery of breath, and it is used figuratively to refer to revival.[63] We understand in context that this passage likely refers to the repentance of the Jewish people preceding the second coming of the Lord, but we also recognize that repentance is an indispensable condition for revival throughout church history (see Acts 2:38; Joel 2:12,28).

Today, God wants His people to experience a fresh outpouring of His Spirit. He wants us to be spiritually refreshed and revived so we can steward what is to follow (i.e., the harvest of souls and transformation of society). The Church needs to return to her first love—to make first things first—in order to move onward with the right posture, the right motives, and the right vision. When we are consumed by our love for Jesus and stay in-tune with the Father's heart, we will be able to partner with the fresh move of the Holy Spirit in this exciting hour in history. Let's contend to see our nation turn back to God as the Church is revived like never before!

Chapter 6

THE HARVEST COMES IN

★ ★ ★ ★ ★

When the Church is revived and has tasted God's glory, the next phase in any true revival is when the harvest comes in. It is necessary for us as Christians to be revived in our spiritual walk with the Lord, but we must also get our nets ready to bring in a great harvest of souls. To see our nation return to God through historic revival, we must contend not just for God's people but for the lost.

From the birth of the Church, we find this same pattern displayed. On the day of Pentecost when the Spirit was poured out, Peter stood up to preach to the crowds, and 3,000 people were saved in one day (Acts 2:41). Among those who were baptized on Pentecost were Jews representing 15 or more language groups and potentially up to 70 nations in the Jewish diaspora.[64] Revival started in Jerusalem, but God intended it to spread to the ends of the earth.

Nations Will Come to Jesus

God's heart is huge, so it is no surprise that He wants to bring in a massive harvest of people to Himself. We see this amazing promise proclaimed by the prophet Isaiah: "Arise, shine; for your light has come, and the glory of the Lord has risen upon you… Nations will come to your light, and kings to the brightness of your rising" (Isaiah 60:1-3). Notice the order of events: The glory comes first (verse 1), and then nations will come to our light (verse 3). We cannot expect nonbelievers to act like believers until they give their hearts to Jesus. In the same way, how can we expect the lost to be revived and come to the church en masse if the church itself is dry and lifeless?

A church during revival prepares the way for hungry souls to encounter the power and presence of God. A church that is dynamic, full of life, and experiencing the glory of God will act like a magnet for lost souls to come in. The world will recognize that something is different about us as we testify about a living Savior. They will hear testimonies sprouting organically from revival, such as dramatic salvations, supernatural healings, angelic visitation, and the like. The testimony of what God has done in our midst will spark faith and hunger in the weary souls looking for spiritual refreshing. The arrival of historic revival will impact communities and, in turn, spread to regions and the entire nation.

The Welsh Revival

The Welsh Revival of 1904 is an example of how the harvest comes in tremendously during true historic revival. As the Church in Wales was starting to be revived by the Holy Spirit, 20,000 people got saved in just five weeks' time. Within the first six months of the revival, 100,000 came to Christ out of Wales' overall population of around 2 million. The press was covering the revival in such detail that many people became followers of Jesus simply after reading about the move of God in their daily newspapers![65] One Welsh minister recounted, "Our young people desert the theater, the football field, and the public-house by the thousand, and flock into every place of worship whose doors are open; and scores of them take part in every way they can to advance the movement."[66]

Evan Roberts, a young minister-in-training, was at the helm of this revival. Through his example we can see that revival starts when we ask the Holy Spirit to search our hearts and mold us. I find it interesting that Evan's main prayer leading up to this move of God was "Bend me." He would pray that every day for years.

As a coal miner, Evan would come home from work, take a bath (which wasn't a common practice in those days), and go to church at Moriah Chapel to pray. The pastor would ask Evan why he was there every day, as there was nothing forcing him to be at church all the time. Evan's response essentially was, "I have to come because I don't know when God is going to show up, and I don't want to miss Him when He does show up." His hunger for the Holy Spirit was incredible.

How hungry are you for revival? Matthew 5:6 says, "Blessed are those who hunger and thirst for righteousness, for they shall be satisfied." Those who are hungry for the things of God are the ones who will be filled. Evan Roberts kept praying, "Bend me! Bend me!" Then suddenly in October 1904, the Holy Spirit came crashing upon him, and the flames of revival spread like wildfire.

A contemporary of Roberts marveled at the way the Welsh Revival was entirely Spirit led. Without any strong sense of organization or human leadership, the revival nevertheless "moves from day to day, week to week, county to county, with matchless precision, with the order of an attacking force... The Sunday-school is having its harvest now. The family altar is having its harvest now.

The teaching of hymns and the Bible among those Welsh hills and valleys is having its harvest now."[67]

The harvest kept growing as Evan Roberts and his youth group actively pursued the Great Commission. After they experienced the power of the Holy Spirit, they would go to every single bar in town and preached the gospel to the people inside. They made a commitment that they were going to preach until they got kicked out—and they did get kicked out! But that didn't stop them. Then they would wait for the patrons to leave the bar so they could share the gospel with them again.

Besides the pubs, Roberts and the youth who were on fire for the Lord would go to the jailhouses and preach the Good News to the prisoners, too. Within half a year, the revival had spread so powerfully that the jails were empty. The police had nothing to do because everyone had gotten saved!

It is recorded that the Christmas season of 1904 was the happiest Christmas of all. [68] Before the revival, the Welsh coal miners would always buy alcohol with their Christmas bonus and get drunk on Christmas Day. But during the Christmas of 1904, the saved miners wanted to go to the church services, and with their Christmas bonuses they decided to buy gifts for their kids for the first time. According to historians, you could walk down the streets in Wales and hear families laughing. Joy was restored to the Welsh families as they were knit together by the love of Jesus. That is what revival looks like! It is the arrival of God's Kingdom, His "righteousness, peace, and joy in the Holy Spirit" (Romans 14:17).

The 1857 Prayer Revival

Another eye-opening example of the harvest coming in is the 1857 Prayer Revival. In the winter of 1857, the northern United States were hit with "a great revival" in the words of Charles Finney, who has been called "the father of modern revivalism." A simple merchant from New York named Jeremiah Lanphier convened the Fulton Street prayer meeting, which would last three years and have a ripple effect spreading revival fire across the globe.

By February 1858, tens of thousands of people were filling New York City's churches and public buildings downtown as they gathered in prayer. The press couldn't help but notice the move of God, so newspapers started providing daily coverage on "The Progress of the Revival." While the public eye was on New York, revival was rapidly extending from state to state. A newspaper article from that season indicated, "There are several New England towns in which not a single adult person can be found unconverted."[69] That same year, revival hit Charleston, North Carolina, under the leadership of John Girardeau and went on non-stop for eight weeks straight, night and day.

At the height of the Prayer Revival, 50,000 souls were getting saved each week. Out of the U.S. population of 30 million, up to 2 million people came to Christ between 1857 and 1859. What an incredible harvest! To put those numbers into perspective, if the same thing happened in America today, it would equate to nearly 20 million souls coming into the Kingdom.

The harvest fields around the world were also ready for the work of the Holy Spirit. In 1859, Ireland and Wales were hit with a wave of revival, and both nations saw 100,000 come to Christ. It is estimated that more than 1 million salvations occurred throughout the United Kingdom. Sweden and Norway likewise embraced the move of the Spirit, and 250,000 people got saved within a year's time. Not only in Europe, but the revival swept across India, the West Indies, Australia, and South Africa.[70]

The Jesus People Movement

Midway through the 20th century, a fresh move of God known as the Jesus People movement brought in a large harvest in America. Before the Jesus movement emerged, the stage was set by the Charismatic Renewal beginning in 1960 with Dennis Bennett in Van Nuys, California. The renewal embraced the baptism and gifts of the Spirit, and it spread especially among Catholics in places like Duquesne, Notre Dame, and Ann Arbor, Michigan. At the same time, a harvest of young people started to come in.

In 1967, revival came flooding in with the outbreak of the Jesus People movement, led by Chuck Smith and Calvary Chapel in Costa Mesa, California. The Jesus People movement led to the salvation of 2 million teenagers by 1971 and would last until 1977. Many of these young converts were hippies who encountered the manifest presence of God and were transformed by the power of the Holy Spirit. By the summer of 1971, *Time* magazine had the words "Jesus Revolution" plastered across its cover. The June 21, 1971 issue of this remarkably secular American magazine contains the following words in the article titled "The New Rebel Cry: Jesus Is Coming":

> "Jesus is alive and well and living in the radical spiritual fervor of a growing number of young Americans who have proclaimed an extraordinary religious revolution in his name. Their message: the Bible is true, miracles happen, God really did love the world that he gave it his only begotten son...."[71]

The article calls the movement "a startling development" in the youth of America, who were "afire with a Pentecostal passion" as they replaced their vices of drugs, sex, and violence with selflessness, purity, and brotherly love.

The flames of revival quickly spread from California all throughout America, particularly the Midwest, and beyond. Making the cover story of the June 30, 1972 issue of *LIFE* magazine, approximately 200,000 Jesus People showed up in Dallas, Texas, for Explo '72, a weeklong event sponsored by Campus Crusade for Christ.[72] With 80,000 daily attendees representing 75 distinct nations, it was "a religious Woodstock" in the words of the late great evangelist Billy Graham, who spoke six times at the crusade.[73]

Due to the wide-reaching effects of the Jesus People movement, somewhere around 20 million people got saved in the revival's wake. I was one of the long-haired "Jesus freaks" who got saved in 1973, and I am so grateful for my revival heritage. When I encountered the radical love of Jesus Christ, I left my old lifestyle of partying and dealing drugs—and was instantly set free from all addictions! (You can read more of my testimony in my books *How to Pray for Healing* and *Spirit-Led Evangelism*.)

When I first got saved, I wanted to hug anybody who moved. I had a burning desire to share the gospel with everyone. I would drive up and down the six-lane highway that I lived on, Georgia Avenue, looking for hitchhikers. In those days, back in the 70s, all of the hippies hitchhiked. So I would pick up the hitchhikers, and once they were trapped in my car, I'd share the gospel with them! I'd lead them to Jesus Christ, bring them to my house, fill up the bathtub, and baptize them the same day they got saved. It was so easy to lead people to the Lord. When someone would come up to me and ask what time it was, I'd reply, "It's time to get saved," and they would give their hearts to Jesus on the spot!

Most of the American pastors in my generation came to Christ during the Jesus People movement. We were all hippies! Among many good friends of mine, I think of Charles Stock, a member of Harvest International Ministry's International Apostolic Team and the founding pastor of Life Center Ministries International in

Harrisburg, Pennsylvania. Charles was one of the multitudes that God called out of hippiedom and set on fire with the Holy Spirit. From the Jesus People days until now, Charles' life has been a testimony of God's faithfulness to carry on the good work that God began in him during a time of incredible harvest.

America Needs Revival

For years I have been asking God, "Where is the revival that You promised me?" In 1984, my wife, Sue, and I moved our family from the Washington D.C. area out to Los Angeles because of a prophetic dream I had in 1982. I still have not yet seen the total fulfillment of that word after more than 38 years. Yes, I have seen God renew and refresh the Church through the Toronto Blessing and the Brownsville Revival, as well as our nightly renewal meetings at Mott Auditorium from 1995 to 1998, but we never saw the harvest coming in en masse. But for the first time since the Jesus People days, I am starting to see signs of the harvest coming in.

As of this writing, we are seeing the harvest come in through revivalists Sean Feucht and Jay Koopman, one of my spiritual sons, as they have been leading the Let Us Worship events throughout America. Since the summer of 2020, they have seen thousands come to know the Lord in over 133 cities and counting.[74] "People are carrying a fire like never before," Jay recounted about what he has witnessed on the West Coast. "They are preaching on airplanes, they are open-air preaching on trains, they are preaching in restaurants, and so it's giving the church this boldness to not just fight for America, but also to win souls and make disciples."[75]

My friend Mario Murillo is another ardent revivalist seeing the harvest come in, especially in California, through his evangelistic tent meetings. Mario's tent crusades are, in the words of journalist Joel Kilpatrick, "one evidence of the arrival of a large-scale move of God that many have expected and prophesied."[76] During a week-long crusade in Sacramento in August 2021, a crowd of 4,000 attended nightly, and hundreds responded to the gospel message at the first night's altar call. In fact, Mario called me before the Sacramento meetings. He said, "Pastor, if we have 200 at our pre-crusade pastors' lunch, it is a great sign. But we had to cut off the lunch at 900 for Sacramento!" Evoking the days when God first called him to be an evangelist, Mario declared, "The Jesus Movement of the new millennium is happening right before your eyes."[77]

My Dream of a Great Harvest

Back in 1982, I was an associate pastor at a church in Maryland, when I had a life-changing dream encounter. On September 2, at 4 o'clock in the morning, a black man appeared to me in my dream. Somehow, I knew that the man was 6 feet 5 inches tall, 300 pounds, without an ounce of fat on his body, like a football player. He said to me, "God is calling you to Los Angeles, for there will be a great harvest."

When I woke up, I heard the words of a song that we often sang at that time, "The time of revival is at hand." I woke up Sue and told her the dream. She immediately bore witness to the fact that it wasn't just a dream, as we felt the manifest presence of God in such a profound way. I'll never forget how we got out of bed, got on our knees, and prayed together. At that time, we didn't know anybody in LA; I had only been there once before, and Sue hadn't ever made the journey to Southern California. We prayed, "Lord, open the door if You want us to go to Los Angeles." I threw a fleece out and said, "Let my pastor initiate this move. I'm not going to say anything. I'm going to ask You, Lord, to have him come to me and say, 'I really feel you need to plant a church. Where would you like to go?'"

Sure enough, six months later my pastor Larry Tomczak, best known for his bestselling book *Clap Your Hands* and now a columnist for Charisma Media, took me out for lunch and said, "I've really been thinking about this for a long time. I feel like I need to ask you, if you were to plant a church, where would you like to go?" Since we were in Rockville and Gaithersburg, Maryland, at the time, he was probably thinking I was going to say some place in our region, like Fairfax or Annandale, Virginia. When I told Larry I wanted to go to Los Angeles, almost 3,000 miles away, he almost fell out of his chair! So I told him the dream, and to make a long story short, he and the other pastors from my church bore witness to what we were sensing. I always like it when there is confirmation from the pastors in a believer's life. We did not just leave independently, but we were sent out from our home congregation.

Thus, in 1984, my family and I moved out to Los Angeles along with Lou Engle and his family. That same year, we planted Abundant Life Church, which we would continue to pastor until 1992. Then in 1994, revival broke out—first hitting Toronto and then Los Angeles. Sue and I decided to open our home for prayer meetings in March of 1994. Around 30 people showed up the first night. By week three, our house was packed with more than 72 people coming to pray. The week after, we rented a friend's church building, and over 300 people showed up. One week later, on April 4, 1994, we officially launched Harvest Rock Church.

Our church was birthed out of a season of revival. In January 1995, renewal meetings began in Mott Auditorium in Pasadena with 2,000 people, as John Arnott came and imparted to us from the Toronto Blessing. That April, our church moved into Mott, and we went on to host protracted meetings five nights per week. By the close of 1995, Harvest Rock Church merged with three other local congregations with distinct backgrounds, demonstrating remarkable unity during the move of God. Our nightly meetings at Mott Auditorium would continue until 1998!

Everyone Got Saved

I find great encouragement in revival history, especially when reading about the harvest coming in. The Hebrides Revival of 1948 comes to mind. According to the Scottish Presbyterian evangelist Duncan Campbell, there was one particular island off of Scotland, the Isle of Lewis, where literally everyone got saved. There was not one person on the island who did not come to Jesus.

To accommodate these believers, every church building was filled four times every day of the week. They had services at 7:30 p.m., 9:30 p.m., 11:30 p.m., and 1:30 a.m. every day. Everyone worked during the daytime, as a strong work ethic was part of their culture, so they provided the services at night. And everyone was only allowed to attend one service per week, because every service was completely packed to capacity.

For a biblical precedent of entire cities getting saved, see the account in Acts 9 where a paralyzed man named Aeneas was dramatically healed during Peter's ministry—"so all who dwelt at Lydda and Sharon saw him and turned to the Lord" (Acts 9:35, NKJV).

What does that kind of revival look like in a city like Los Angeles with 4 million people? What will the end-time harvest look like?

Signposts to a Billion-Soul Harvest

In 1983, a prophet in Kansas City named Bob Jones gave an extraordinary word. He prophesied a Billion-Soul Harvest that would begin in the United States, and he said that three signs would take place in America before this harvest begins.

First, Bob said an "abortion pill" would be invented. Today, we know this as the "morning-after pill." Second, he prophesied that same-sex marriage would be legalized in America. When Bob said this in 1983, everyone thought he was a heretic! It seemed highly improbable at the time, but as you know, in June of 2015, our Supreme Court legalized same-sex marriage. Third, Bob prophesied something really bizarre: A watch would be invented that would be the best-selling watch in China, where people would be able to listen to worship music as they work in the rice paddies. In 2015, the Apple Watch was invented, allowing anyone in the world to carry worship music conveniently on their wrist. Thus, all three signs were fulfilled by the end of 2015.

From that point onward, the prophetic signposts started appearing more frequently. In January 2016, James Goll came to our Prophetic Conference and prophesied a "West Coast Rumble," saying that revival is going to break out from Tijuana all the way to Vancouver —a tsunami wave of revival that will hit America. Around the same time, Loren Cunningham, a tremendous man of God who founded YWAM (Youth With A Mission), visited our church and shared with us an open vision that he had in 2015. It is important to note that Loren has only had two visions in 60 years of ministry, so it is not like he is sharing about visions all the time. This was a very strong word that was impressed upon him. In the vision, Loren saw a huge tsunami wave crash upon the West Coast of the United States. When he asked the Lord what it was, the Lord answered, "It is going to be the greatest revival that America has ever experienced."

On April 9, 2016, another prophetic signpost was reached with the Azusa Now prayer gathering held in the Los Angeles Memorial Coliseum. To give proper context, we must go back to the days of Mott Auditorium in Pasadena, when my daughter's best friend, Christina, prophesied that stadiums would be filled and that Mott was too small for the coming move of God—"Stadium Christianity." (I write more about this in my book *When Heaven Comes Down*.)

She also saw Vince Lombardi in a vision; since she was a young girl from the Philippines, she didn't know anything about who he was. What could that mean? The first Super Bowl, won by Vince Lombardi and the Green Bay Packers, was played in the LA Coliseum. My dear friend Lou Engle was there when Christina prophesied these things in the mid-1990s, and he prophetically brought the pieces together when he spearheaded the Azusa Now event in the spring of 2016. Marking the 110th anniversary of the Azusa Street Revival, Azusa Now was a phenomenal gathering with around 60,000 attendees praying together in the rain. In my opinion, after organizing the first 7 events for TheCall and participating in around 25 of them, Azusa Now was the most powerful and significant one.

A few months after Azusa Now, in August 2016, Cindy Jacobs was at our annual HIM Global Summit when she prophesied, "The Fourth Great Awakening has just begun." As someone who loves church history, I recognized that "the Fourth Great Awakening" is monumental in significance. We know the First and Second Great Awakenings happened in 1738 and 1801. There is debate about the Third Great Awakening, but I want to submit to you that it took place in 1906 with the Azusa Street Revival. In my spirit I was in full agreement with this prophecy. Cindy went on to prophesy California Dreamin, a church-planting and discipleship initiative that we ended up launching under HIM in December that following year.

As all these prophetic words started to flow together, it became incredibly clear that we are in a season of revival. On February 2, 2020, another piece of the prophetic puzzle fell into place when the Kansas City Chiefs made an amazing comeback to win Super Bowl LIV. This was significant because Bob Jones told a number of people, including James Goll and Shawn Bolz, that one of the sign-posts to the coming Billion-Soul Harvest would be when Kansas City wins the Super Bowl, which they hadn't done since 1969.[78]

We are living in the *kairos* moment to see the Billion-Soul Harvest come in. Even though we have the promise of revival, we are not going to be passive about it. God prophetically gave Israel the Promised Land of Canaan, but they had to wage warfare to take it. In the same way, we must appropriate the promises of God by taking action. We are going to plant new churches and start new satellite congregations, by the grace of God, to the best of our ability. We are going to preach the gospel in our cities with signs and wonders following. Yes, a great harvest is coming—but you and I have to go after it!

Chapter 7

SOCIETY IS TRANSFORMED

★ ★ ★ ★ ★

In any historic revival, first the Church is revived, and second, a harvest of souls comes in. The third necessary component of historic revival is that society is transformed. When the transformation of a nation takes place, we know that revival has truly come.

The First Great Awakening

The best illustration of this principle is the Great Awakening, which began in England in 1738. The great evangelist George Whitefield and the apostle John Wesley were key figures in this revival. Whitefield was a brilliant Oxford graduate and a phenomenal preacher. Wesley, who is personally my favorite figure from the First Great Awakening, started the Methodist denomination by planting all these class groups that ended up becoming churches.

But you have to understand the backdrop for this move of God:

Great Britain was decadent and dark at that time. You might think of everyone as being modest and having proper manners like the Victorian Age, but that occurred *after* the Great Awakening, not before. In England, the time that preceded the Great Awakening was called the "Gin Age" or the "Gin Craze."

Before it became popular in the late 1680s, gin was rare and expensive. Most Englishmen were used to drinking beer, and so were the women, up to a certain point. Yet the English alehouses had primarily catered to men. Gin, which was new and exotic and metropolitan, didn't have any of these old associations. There were no rules around gin. Once it came on the scene, gin took England by storm. Due to the agricultural revolution, gin was cheaper than beer and so easy to make that people started making it in their own homes as an extra revenue source. One out of every four houses in London became a gin house. There were no social norms about who could drink it, when you could drink it, or how much of it you could drink. It is significant to note that the gin back then was twice as potent as it is today.

As a result, England became a nation of alcoholics overnight. The unemployment rate skyrocketed, as people could not function at work because they were so drunk. With joblessness and poverty came a heavy increase in crime. You could not walk through London without getting mugged. It was a dangerous time and people didn't want to be out in public during that period. Many women became prostitutes to finance their alcoholism, and some even sold their daughters into the sex trade. Pedophilia was also off the charts. There were even accounts of people fornicating in Hyde Park in the open air. Such was the state of Great Britain that served as the setting for the First Great Awakening.

In stark contrast with this dark backdrop of English history, George Whitefield started to open-air preach to the coal miners of

Bristol in 1738. One of the heralds of this revival, Whitefield was an articulate preacher of the gospel and had a powerful voice. His voice was so strong that he was able to preach to a multitude of 30,000 people that had gathered in one location, and without any means of amplification, his words were heard with clarity to the furthest edge of the crowd.[79]

Whitefield's main message was that you must simply be born again. This is something that we take for granted today, but it was a radical statement to make back then. In Whitefield's day, most people thought that they were Christian because they were born into a Christian home and were part of the Church of England. But through Whitefield's preaching, the simplicity of the gospel was being reintroduced to Great Britain and hearts were coming alive to God.

Wilberforce and the Abolition of Slavery

In 1760, a young man named William Wilberforce got saved at the age of 27. Born into an aristocratic home, Wilberforce had a Cambridge education and was only 5 feet 3 inches tall. (I like to mention his height because it shows that God can use short people, including me!) While serving in Parliament, Wilberforce had an encounter with the Lord that changed his life's trajectory. His faith was influenced by George Whitefield and the Methodist movement, and his mentor was the seasoned John Newton, a former slave trader who wrote the famous hymn "Amazing Grace."

Following his conversion experience, Wilberforce initially doubted whether he was meant to remain in politics. In time, though, his calling became clear. Wilberforce felt led by God to pursue two main goals. The first of these was the abolition of slavery.

As a member of Parliament, Wilberforce was persistent in presenting bills every year intending to abolish the slave trade. But to realize that goal, the abolitionists would have to overcome major hurdles, not the least of which was the heavy economic toll that abolition would demand of the British Empire.

During that period, England had a monopoly on the slave trade and owned over half of the slave ships in the world. The British Crown had bought out the Spaniards and the Portuguese and had the exclusive rights to buy slaves from Africa and sell them to the United States. The slave trade was the number-one source of income for Great Britain. Think about that: Entire towns were built on the slave trade money. Even though most people in England thought slavery was wrong, they weren't willing to pass a bill to end the slave trade because of the love of money. There was a stronghold tied to greed at the heart of the nation.

Everyone wants to see society transformed, but what does that look like? By the close of the 18th century, William Wilberforce was inextricably connected to an incredible network of leaders called the Clapham Group (whom we met in an earlier chapter). The group's members united around their strong desire to fight for biblical justice in their nation, and they would meet every night to strategize how to obliterate the slave trade and slavery in the British Empire. Representing a variety of vocations and skillsets, the Clapham Circle invested their time, energy, and money into mobilizing people to vote for members of Parliament who were abolitionists.

It takes hard work to win an election and to disciple a nation. But through the political process, the abolitionists started gaining ground in Parliament, and they were practically all Evangelical Christians. For 11 years straight, bill after bill was defeated. Then on February 23, 1807, they finally had enough support to pass the Act for the Abolition of the Slave Trade. On March 25, King George III signed the bill, officially banning the African slave trade in the British Empire. This timing was remarkable when we take into account that U.S. President Thomas Jefferson, just three weeks earlier, on March 2 had signed into law the Act Prohibiting Importation of Slaves. We must also remember that the Second Great Awakening by now was in full swing in America. Thus, America and Britain became the first two nations in the world to ban the slave trade—in the wake of experiencing historic revival.

Invigorated by this long-awaited victory, Wilberforce and his companions continued to pursue transformation and reformation in their generation. They were formidable forces for good, "engaged in an antislavery public opinion campaign unprecedented in English history."[80] On the road toward banishing slavery from the entire Empire, the abolitionists presented to the House of Commons nearly 1 million signatures on 800 petitions—representing 10% of the country's population.[81]

Wilberforce did not only focus on the abolition of slavery, which of course was the central piece, but his second goal was the "Reformation of Manners." This had nothing to do with table manners, but rather an effort to restore morality to England. In 1787, the words of young Wilberforce moved King George III and the archbishop of Canterbury to "issue an official proclamation in favor of improved morals and better enforcement of existing laws against vices such as gambling, drunkenness, impiety, Sabbath breaking, prostitution, and profanity."[82] The resulting Proclamation Society gained support from across the social spectrum and helped pave the way for later efforts pursued by Clapham. Indeed, Wilberforce and his companions championed numerous causes and societies, related to education for the poor, foreign and domestic missions, humanitarian aid, hospital care reform, prison reform, and even a society combatting the cruel treatment of animals.

In their relatively small numbers, the members of Clapham wielded unparalleled influence on English society in the early

1800s. Their diverse campaigns helped to imbue the nation with a newfound sense of compassion for the lowly and disenfranchised, as each Claphamite proactively moved in their sphere of influence spurring on others toward acts of good will. The reforms sparked by the Clapham Circle effectively "set the tone for the coming Victorian age with its emphases on religion, morality, family, and duty."[83] Thus, the cultural and political makeup of England would be reshaped as a direct result of the soul of the nation being spiritually awakened.

You see, revival always brings about social transformation. We must bear in mind that this transformation may take a long time to be fully realized. For example, the Great Awakening broke out in 1738, but slavery was finally made illegal in the British Empire in 1833. The battle for abolition was a long uphill battle, but it was well worth the struggle.

Did you know that William Wilberforce died just three days after Parliament passed the Slavery Abolition Act? How wonderful it must have been for him to see the fruit of his lifelong effort to see slavery abolished right before he went to be with the Lord. Wilberforce has an incredible story, and he is one of my heroes because of the amount of transformation he brought to the world. (I encourage you to read Eric Metaxas' book *Amazing Grace* to get to know William Wilberforce even better.)

Ending Slavery in America

In the United States of America, it was also the Evangelicals who brought about the abolition movement and saw society transformed in the wake of spiritual revival. In the fall of 1821, a young lawyer named Charles Finney had a powerful encounter with the Holy Spirit, and as a result was used mightily by God to spark revival in the days that followed. In 1851, Finney became president of Oberlin

College in Ohio, where he used this platform to advocate social reform, most notably the abolition of slavery.

By this time, the Methodist movement had become America's largest Protestant denomination. From the year 1780 onward, the Methodists explicitly held to the truth that "slavery is contrary to the laws of God, man, and nature—hurtful to society; contrary to the dictates of conscience and pure religion, and doing that which we would not others should do to us and ours."[84] Although Methodism experienced a split into north and south, revival flames were kindled all around the U.S. due to a lively return to the movement's original Wesleyan roots. The Wesleyan Methodist Church of America, officially formed in 1843, recognized its unified call to vehemently oppose slavery. After all, John Wesley himself had labeled slavery "the sum of all villainies."

As we saw in the last chapter, the 1857 Prayer Revival was the primary revival that hit Northern America during this time, bringing in a massive harvest of souls into God's Kingdom. Soon, though, the issue of slavery would come to a head as the first shots of the Civil War were fired in the spring of 1861. Charles P. Schmitt writes, "Discerning Church historians are not slow to sense in the devastating ravages of the Civil War the judgments of a holy God against the abominations of slavery."[85]

Nearly halfway through the embittered national conflict, President Abraham Lincoln issued the historic Emancipation Proclamation, releasing a clarion call to put an end to slavery. Indeed, Lincoln had a keen sense of how slavery was a grievous sin in the eyes of God and how America desperately needed reformation. In his second inaugural address, on March 4, 1865, President Lincoln proclaimed:

> "Fondly do we hope, fervently do we pray, that this
> mighty scourge of war may speedily pass away. Yet,

if God wills that it continue… until every drop of
blood drawn with the lash shall be paid by another
drawn with the sword, as was said three thousand
years ago, so still it must be said 'the judgments of
the Lord are true and righteous altogether.'"[86]

By April 9, 1865, when the Confederates surrendered and the
war finally ended, America had lost over 630,000 of her sons to
bloodshed. In the wake of such a catastrophic chapter in American
history, the way was paved for the passing of the 13th Amendment in
December 1865, which fully abolished slavery in our nation. Within
the next five years, the 14th and 15th Amendments to the Constitution
were ratified to declare civil rights for every individual born in the
United States—including former slaves—and to affirm voting rights
for men of all races.

Though it came at a high price, the social transformation that
took place after the Civil War turned a new page in American
history. Ultimately, it created momentum for the emerging women's
suffrage movement, which secured women's right to vote in 1920
thanks to the 19th Amendment, and the epochal civil rights movement of the 1950s and 1960s.

Continuing to Fight for Transformation

We have seen throughout history that when a massive harvest comes
in, societies are transformed. There are numerous other examples, including the Welsh Revival of 1904-1905, when entire communities
in Wales saw radical transformation as souls were coming to Christ
and starting to do life according to the Spirit. I want to submit to you
that God desires to do that again—but on an even larger scale.

When we study reformation and transformation, we are talking
about change taking place over the course of decades or even a

century. Today, we have such a short-term bent and we want everything *now*: Instagram, In-N-Out Burger, microwaved meals, etc. We have it embedded into our culture that we are always in such a hurry. But in the Kingdom of God, we often have to give up our own timetable and submit to God's timing.

In Acts 2:17, when Peter stood up on the day of Pentecost, he quoted the prophet Joel: "'And it shall be in the last days,' God says, 'that I will pour forth of My Spirit on all mankind.'" It was almost 2,000 years ago when the apostle said those words, but ever since the first Pentecost, we have been in "the last days." Something we must be careful about is not to project our understanding of time onto God's timing. The Bible says, "But do not let this one fact escape your notice, beloved, that with the Lord one day is like a thousand years, and a thousand years like one day" (2 Peter 3:8). We are still living in the last days, and I believe we are going to see a mighty outpouring of God's Spirit in this generation.

When I first moved to California in the 1980s, Pasadena was the murder capital of Los Angeles. It wasn't Watts or South Central, but Pasadena. Because of the gang wars between the Bloods and the Crypts, Pasadena was averaging 365 homicides per year. In 1995 when the Lord told our church to go into protracted meetings, I didn't fully understand then that by meeting five nights a week for three years, we were cleansing the spiritual atmosphere over Pasadena.

Today the murder rate in our city is next to nothing, as the gangs completely moved out of Pasadena. The downtown area of Old Pasadena was literally revived. Back in 1984, Old Pasadena was a dilapidated, run-down, red-light district of the city, with adult bookstores competing with each other. Now the area is a major tourist attraction with high-end stores and restaurants, and no prostitutes or adult bookstores to be found.

There are many other testimonies I could mention, like a major cult based in Pasadena called the Worldwide Church of God, which experienced revival and turned into an Evangelical church. Critics will say that these things are a coincidence, but I believe that through our protracted services, we saw a measure of transformation in our city.

The Church in America today is fighting a spiritual battle to transform our nation. In the book of Joshua, we see principles that we can apply to our generation, for those who will turn to the Lord with our whole hearts and follow His call. In Joshua 1:3, the Lord told Joshua, "Every place on which the sole of your foot treads, I have given it to you, just as I spoke to Moses." Even though God had promised Israel the land of Canaan, God's people still had to fight over every inch of territory in front of them. It wasn't an easy task.

Yet despite the opposition, Joshua led the Israelites into battle, and God supernaturally led them to victory over their enemies. In that same spirit, I believe we need to contend in prayer for revival and take action to bring reformation and transformation to our nation.

Peter Wagner once said, "The harvest is among the poor, but transformation takes place through kings." What exactly does this mean? As we know, transformation can take place through geopolitical leaders, including actual monarchs. So, it does matter who is in office, as our political leaders have great opportunity—and great responsibility—to steward their authority and transform society for good. Every election matters, and we need to elect people who have biblical values.

But the point I want to focus on here is that all believers are kings and priests before God (see Revelation 1:6, 5:10, and 1 Peter 2:9). There is no difference between the "minister" behind the pulpit and the marketplace leader sitting in the pew. It is time for all of us as believers to "roll up our sleeves" and get to work in reforming our state and our nation.

Chances are you are being called into the marketplace, into one of the seven mountains of culture. You may be more effective and anointed working in the government or business mountain, compared to the traditional role of working in a church. This value of transforming all areas of society is central to each of the ministries I am involved in. We must continually remind ourselves of this calling because it takes the renewal of our thinking in order to see the transformation of our lives, and ultimately our sphere of influence.

If you are a follower of Jesus Christ, you are key to the transformation of your nation!

PART 3:

CONDITIONS FOR HISTORIC REVIVAL

★ ★ ★ ★ ★

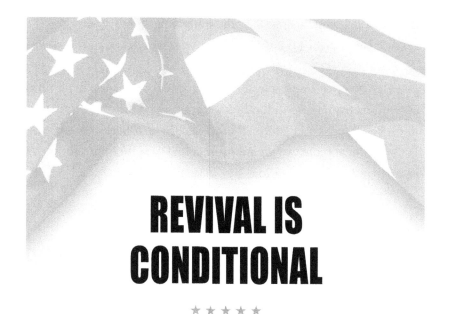

REVIVAL IS CONDITIONAL

★ ★ ★ ★ ★

Did you know that revival thrives in a unique ecosystem?

So far, we have learned valuable lessons from church history by identifying several keys to stewarding revival well. We have also identified the three main characteristics of historic revivals, seeing how major moves of God throughout history have manifested in common ways. Now that we can recognize the effects of a history-making revival once it is already in full swing, it is time to ask the question: What are the conditions that will set a historic revival into motion?

Renowned 18th-century theologian Jonathan Edwards said that if you want to experience revival, there must be "explicit agreement, visible union, and extraordinary prayer."[87] As I have studied many powerful moves of God throughout church history, I agree with Edwards' assessment of revival. At the same time, I want to submit my personal conclusion that the following three conditions are essential for revival: (1) *unity*, (2) *extraordinary prayer*, and (3) *radical obedience*.

The book of Acts sets the perfect precedence for these three conditions leading up to the first outpouring of the Holy Spirit, the day of Pentecost. Let's look at each one, first in Scripture and then in church history, as we glean insights that will fuel our faith to see historic revival in our nation.

Chapter 8

UNITY

★ ★ ★ ★ ★

There is exponential power in unity. This is true in the natural as well as in the spiritual. The Word of God says, "One will chase a thousand, and two will put ten thousand to flight" (Deuteronomy 32:30). One horse can pull 6 tons of weight, but two horses harnessed together can pull 32 tons! We were created to live and thrive in unity, for that is where God commands His blessing. We are also called to contend together in unity for revival.

Unity and Apostolic Alignment

Psalm 133 is one of the shortest psalms, and yet it is one of most powerful because it talks about a specific type of unity that is key for God's people. I believe that Psalm 133 is very apostolic and that it expresses a truth about apostolic alignment. As one of the "songs of ascent" (Psalms 120-134), this psalm was sung by Jews during their uphill journey to Jerusalem, to attend the three annual feasts mentioned in Deuteronomy 16:16. The Levitical priests also sang Psalm 133 as they walked up the temple steps. They would take one step and sing one song of ascent, and then take another step and sign another song of ascent. That is why these psalms are so short.

Psalm 133 says, "Behold, how good and how pleasant it is for brothers to live together in unity! It is like the precious oil on the head, running down upon the beard, as on Aaron's beard, the oil which ran down upon the edge of his robes. It is like the dew of Hermon coming down upon the mountains of Zion; for the Lord commanded the blessing there—life forever."

Why is Aaron highlighted in this passage? By the time this psalm was written, Aaron had been dead for hundreds of years. Psalm 133 mentions Aaron because he was the first high priest appointed by the Lord, and the high priest is a type of an apostle in the Old Testament. As the priests were praying this psalm each year, they were reaffirming their commitment to the current high priest during that period of their priestly service.

Thus, Aaron represents whoever the high priest is in the apostolic period of the Church. Why is that important? The book of Hebrews draws a distinct connection between the high priest and an apostle. Hebrews 3:1 states, "Therefore, holy brethren, partakers of the heavenly calling, consider the Apostle and High Priest of our confession, Christ Jesus" (NKJV). Here we clearly see that Jesus is the Apostle, and He is the High Priest. This verse shows that a high priest is like the apostle.

This has a lot of ramifications. In the context of Psalm 133, God is saying, "As you align yourself as a priest to whoever the high priest is, there is going to be a commanded blessing." Alignment brings about that blessing.

As mentioned earlier, revival spreads through an aligned apostolic network. This is a network that is aligned with the vision and values of the apostolic leader—for example, William Seymour, the Clapham Group aligned with William Wilberforce, John Wesley,

Brother Xi in China, and others. I believe that God is calling the Church to come into alignment and unity to see revival but also to create a wineskin for the new wine (see Matthew 9:17).

Unity and Revival in Acts

In the opening of Acts, we see remarkable unity displayed among the members of the early Church in the days leading up to Pentecost. After witnessing Christ ascend into heaven, the 11 Apostles stayed in Jerusalem as they eagerly awaited "the promise of the Father" that Jesus spoke of. Acts 1:14 gives us a glimpse into the unity of Christ's followers in their upper room gathering: "These all continued with *one accord* in prayer and supplication, with the women and Mary the mother of Jesus, and with His brothers" (NKJV).

The Greek word *homothumadon*, translated here as "one accord," is a very important word. It emphasizes unity and is used specifically in connection with revival and the move of the Spirit in Acts. The 120 believers in the upper room were not just in the same physical location; they were in the same place in the spirit. Their hearts were woven together as they were all in one accord.

God loves to see His people united. He so wants to release miracles, answers to prayer, and revival as His Church makes it her priority to come together in unity and prayer. It was that type of environment where the Holy Spirit was welcomed to fall on the day of Pentecost. As a result of their unity, revival broke out in the upper room in Acts 2:1-4:

> "When the day of Pentecost had come, they were all together in one place. And suddenly a noise like a violent rushing wind came from heaven, and it filled the whole house where they were sitting. And tongues that looked like fire appeared to them,

distributing themselves, and a tongue rested on each one of them. And they were all filled with the Holy Spirit and began to speak with different tongues, as the Spirit was giving them the ability to speak out."

Pentecost itself was absolutely astonishing, as 3,000 people got saved in just that one day. But the move of the Holy Spirit was only beginning!

In the days following Pentecost, the Church was marked by continual signs of the supernatural and unprecedented harmony. They were constantly fellowshipping with one another, praying together, and witnessing miracles take place by the power of the Holy Spirit (Acts 2:42-43). Their unity was so remarkable that it led to extraordinary generosity: "Now all who believed were together, and had all things in common, and sold their possessions and goods, and divided them among all, as anyone had need" (Acts 2:44-45, NKJV).

The next appearance of the word *homothumadon* is in Acts 2:46, where we read how the world's first band of Holy Spirit revivalists "continued daily with *one accord* in the temple" (NKJV). In the very next verse we see that "the Lord added to the church daily those who were being saved" (Acts 2:47, NKJV). In the wake of this incredible unity, unbelievers were getting saved every single day as the Spirit was moving among the Church. Talk about church growth!

The narrative continues with ever-increasing revival paralleling the exceptional unity in the Body of Christ. In Acts 3, a noteworthy miracle created a stir as a man crippled from birth was dramatically healed outside the temple gates. As a result, Peter and John preached the gospel to a large crowd, and the harvest came pouring in with 5,000 people getting saved that same day (Acts 4:4).

As is the case with many revivals, the move of the Holy Spirit also provoked criticism and backlash from others. After the Jewish religious leaders threatened Peter and John, we again find the exact same dynamic of united prayer as the believers gathered together to listen to Peter and John's testimony. Acts 4:24 (NKJV) tells us, "So when they heard that, they raised their voice to God with *one accord*" (*homothumadon*) as they lifted up a fiery prayer of revival.

What was the result of their unity? "At that moment the earth shook beneath them, causing the building they were in to tremble. Each one of them was filled with the Holy Spirit, and they proclaimed the word of God with unrestrained boldness" (Acts 4:31, TPT). Completely unified, the believers were super-charged with faith and with the Holy Spirit even as their physical surroundings were shaken by the raw power of God.

Unity at Azusa Street

So many powerful moments in church history are marked by unity among God's people. In the first decade of the 20th century, the Azusa Street Revival was a particularly shining example of what unity in the Body of Christ looks like as the Holy Spirit is being poured out.

Any account of Azusa Street would be incomplete without William Seymour. With humble beginnings as a son of slaves in Louisiana, Seymour was a black Holiness pastor who learned about the baptism of the Holy Spirit under Charles Parham, another key figure in the days of the emerging Pentecostal movement. After attending a short-term Bible school held by Parham at the start of 1906, Seymour was invited to Los Angeles to pastor a new Holiness congregation. His first sermon emphasizing the baptism of the Spirit and speaking in tongues, which caused the church leadership to immediately dismiss Seymour from his post.

Despite the initial setback, Seymour wouldn't relent from his quest for more of the Spirit. He had such an incredible hunger for

God that he increased his time in prayer from five to seven hours a day![88] He was intent on receiving the gift of tongues and the power and infilling of the Holy Spirit, which he had yet to experience first-hand. Seymour found willing vessels to partner with his hunger in Richard and Ruth Asberry, who welcomed him to pray and minister in their home at 214 Bonnie Brae Street. This is where the Holy Spirit fell powerfully on April 9, 1906.

Carl Brumback describes the glorious beginning to the outpour-ing on Bonnie Brae Street: "As though hit by a bolt of lightning, the entire company was knocked from their chairs to the floor. Seven began to speak in divers kinds of tongues and to magnify God... Soon it was noised over the city that God was pouring out His Spirit. White people joined the colored saints and also joined the ranks of those filled with the Holy Ghost."[89]

By mid-April the swelling numbers of God-chasers necessitated the strategic move to an empty church building at 312 Azusa Street, where services would continue for 1,000 consecutive days.[90] As people flocked to Azusa Street to encounter God together, they experienced racial unity that was unprecedented for the time, and the glory of God came.

Harvey Cox explains, "The interracial character of the growing congregation on Azusa Street was indeed a kind of miracle. It was, after all, 1906, a time of growing, not diminishing, racial separation everywhere else. But many visitors reported that in the Azusa Street revival blacks and whites and Asians and Mexicans sang and prayed together. Seymour was recognized as the pastor. But there were both black and white deacons, and both black and white women... were exhorters and healers."[91]

During the height of the revival from 1906 to 1909, Azusa Street was experiencing the reality of Christians' call to unity in Galatians 3:28: "There is neither Jew nor Greek, there is neither slave nor free, there is neither male nor female; for you are all one in Christ Jesus." Frank Bartleman, a journalist from the Holiness movement who participated in the early days of the revival, put it this way: "The 'color line' was washed away in the blood."[92]

Seymour would later reflect on the way that unity preceded the powerful move of the Spirit: "I can say, through the power of the Spirit, that wherever God can get a people that will come together in one accord and one mind in the Word of God, the baptism of the Holy Ghost will fall upon them, like as at Cornelius' house." [93] The waves of the revival kept spreading, both throughout America and globally. The racial reconciliation, equality, and integration that characterized the Azusa Street Revival eventually resounded further into American history in the 1960s, when the civil rights movement sparked new legislation helping abolish the racial divide in our nation.

Keeping the Unity of the Spirit

I had a vivid dream in 2008. I was standing on the shores of a beautiful lake with my friend Mike Bickle, the founder of the International House of Prayer. The sun was going down and the sky was a brilliant purple-red color. Mike pointed his finger over the lake and asked, "Do you see that huge angel over the lake?" I told him, "No." He said, "Just keep looking," still pointing in the same direction.

Suddenly, I saw an enormous angel where Mike was pointing at, and this angel had a large net in his hands. As soon as I saw this angel, thousands of angels appeared at once, and all of them were holding a net or four angels were each holding a corner of a net. At the same time, the angels went into the lake and came right out with their nets filled with fish. I knew in my dream that the harvest angels were released (see Matthew 13:39). Then I heard the Lord say in a loud, resounding voice, "Make every effort to keep the unity of the

Spirit through the bond of peace!" (Ephesians 4:3, NIV).

I don't know why Mike was standing next to me. He could be representing the prophetic movement and I, the apostolic. Or it could be that God wants us to move in unity even if our theology is different (not that it is between the two of us; Mike and I would agree to almost everything pertaining to the Kingdom). Whatever the dream means, I do know that God wants us to work at ("make every effort") to walk in unity and love with one another. I believe that as of this writing, the Billion-Soul Harvest has begun! But we must deal with the root issues that cause disunity.

Laying an Ax to the Following Unity Killers

First, we must address doctrinal differences. My appeal here is that there are always going to be doctrinal differences on secondary doctrinal issues. If the major orthodox beliefs are the same (e.g. the divinity of Jesus, etc.), I believe that we can work together and come together in unity and prayer.

I am learning that having been part of the unity movement since 1992, what is more important than doctrine is having a united vision and having united values. I think different streams and denominations can come together over the vision of seeing revival and reformation in one's nation. Seeing one's nation reformed will mean having a measure of the following values restored. This is not an exhaustive list, but it is a list of values that I believe we can advocate with our brothers and sisters in Christ as we seek greater unity among different denominations.

1. First is a pro-life value leading to reformation as reflected in the pro-life legislation being passed in the USA. This begins with *Roe v. Wade* being overturned, resulting in the states passing pro-life laws to outlaw abortion on a state-by-state level. Along with Evangelical believers

being pro-life, we have a major concern for helping the poor, the single parent, the marginalized and vulnerable members of our society at every stage of development and in every condition—including the unborn, the disabled, and the dependent.

2. Next, we want to emphasize the value of having religious freedom. This is to enjoy the freedom to worship in person —not having the State interfere with the free exercise thereof.

3. Personal freedom is also an important value. As of this writing, the political leader of our nation has ordered a vaccine mandate for every federal worker, and then he took the next step to mandate public companies of 100 or more workers to enforce that they must all be vaccinated, or the companies face fines. Unfortunately, companies are enforcing the vaccine mandate by firing people who refuse to get the vaccine. These egregious and totalitarian decrees coming from the government and woke companies must be resisted by all who believe in personal freedom. The issue is not the vaccine but the government forcing people to get the vaccine. We can unite believers around the value of personal freedom.

4. Another value is the biblical value of family, whereby we define marriage as between a man and a woman (see Genesis 2:24).

5. We also can unite over our biblical understanding of one's identity as male or female (see Genesis 1:27), and reject the notion that you can choose your gender depending on what you are thinking or feeling like you want to do

that day.

6. Finally, we need to come together to pursue the unity between Jew and Gentile as reflected in Jesus' High Priestly prayer in John 17. Jesus prayed for divine oneness among His Jewish disciples and "also for those who believe in Me through their word"—that is, Gentiles that would come to salvation (see verses 20-23). Indeed, Jesus went to the cross not only to offer us forgiveness but to establish peace between Jews and Gentiles by creating "in Himself one new man from the two" (Ephesians 2:15, NKJV). According to John 17:21, this unified relationship is a catalytic key to seeing a global harvest of souls—"so that the world may believe" that Jesus is the Messiah.[94] As we get nearer to the second coming of the Lord, we are being called to a greater demonstration of love between Jewish believers and Gentile believers in Jesus (see John 13:34-35).

Other things that divide the Church are what I call "carnal, fleshy issues," like jealousy, the spirit of competition, pride, selfish ambition, and the like. We must crucify the flesh if we want to be followers of Jesus (see Galatians 5:24), and we can't let another person's greater gifts or sphere of ministry cause us to shy back from unity because of these carnal issues. We need to repent and see that God values unity to the point that He devotes a whole chapter of the Bible—John 17—to pray that we would be one as the Father, Son, and Holy Spirit are one.

We must see that we are not in competition with one another, but we are competing against the enemy. We must unite if we want to see His Kingdom come in power and bring about the transformation of nations that we are all longing for.

Chapter 9

EXTRAORDINARY PRAYER

★ ★ ★ ★ ★

"Before God sends revival,
He first begins to mobilize His saints in prayer."
– A.T. Pierson

I strongly believe that in order for any revival to take place, extraordinary prayer must be present as the foundation. Church history proves that the lives of revivalists are always defined by the following words from Scripture: "The effective, fervent prayer of a righteous man [or woman] avails much" (James 5:16, NKJV). Brian Simmons' *The Passion Translation* says it this way: "Tremendous power is released through the passionate, heartfelt prayer of a godly believer!"

Extraordinary Prayer and Revival in Acts

The Holy Spirit always falls in answer to prayer. In the book of Acts, we find the first two conditions for revival often appearing hand-in-hand. Before revival broke out on the day of Pentecost, the members of the early Church, bound together in unity, were dedicating themselves to extraordinary prayer. I like how *The Passion Translation* describes the fervent prayer that we encounter in the upper room: "All of them were united in prayer, gripped with one passion, interceding night and day" (Acts 1:14).

Peter Wagner called this the most powerful prayer meeting in history. After all, this was the prayer meeting that birthed Pentecost! Just imagine the prayers that the apostles prayed during the 10 days between the day of Ascension and the day of Pentecost. They were the first to experience what it truly means to be born again. They had witnessed firsthand the resurrection power of God as their Risen Lord and Savior "proved to them with many convincing signs that he had been resurrected" (Acts 1:3, TPT). And they had just been commissioned by Jesus Himself to preach His Good News and make disciples of all nations (Matthew 28:18-20). Whatever these prayers sounded like, you can be sure they were extraordinary!

The prayers leading up to the day of Pentecost had timely, prophetic significance, as they were in preparation for a great spiritual harvest. Pentecost was known as the Feast of Weeks, but it was also called the Feast of Harvest, for it marked the day when the Jewish people were to take the firstfruits of the annual wheat harvest and present them to the Lord (see Exodus 34:22). In Peter Wagner's commentary on the Book of Acts, we find this valuable insight:

> "What is it that the disciples were praying for 'with one accord in one place'? They were praying for the Holy Spirit to come upon them and impart to them

the power needed for carrying the gospel of the kingdom across all conceivable barriers. They were praying that God would send them forth as laborers into the harvest fields of the day."[95]

As the 120 in the upper room anticipated an incomparable gift, the baptism of the Holy Spirit, they devoted themselves to pray indefinitely. They knew the Holy Spirit was going to come, but they did not know when He would come. They had no clue what the baptism of the Holy Spirit would look and sound like. Nevertheless, they were determined to pray until the Holy Spirit fell.

In the wake of their unity—mingled with extraordinary prayer—the 120 were rewarded with a history-shaping encounter with the supernatural power of the Holy Spirit (see Acts 2:1-11).

Extraordinary Prayer in Church History

Alice Smith writes in her book *Beyond the Veil*, "Burning, believing, prevailing, persuading, persevering, intimate prayer always precedes a move of God."[96] I couldn't agree more.

Extraordinary prayer is a core condition for historic revival because one of the greatest keys to bringing God's will to the earth is prayer. Francis Frangipane said, "If we will gain God's greatest blessings, we must embrace His highest purpose." I believe that God's highest purpose is to advance His Kingdom with His love and His power, and we begin that process through prayer.

The 100-Year Prayer Meeting

Throughout all of church history, there have been many significant times marked by united, extraordinary prayer. The Moravian Church, who we met in an earlier chapter, is a prime example. There was initially much division at Herrnhut due to many different cultures, languages, churches, and economic stress. But everything changed in 1727.

Count Zinzendorf established small groups of two, three, or more individuals who would gather regularly to pray. On August 12, 1727, they had an all-night prayer meeting. The next day, they had a "love feast," and they covenanted together to walk in unity and love. On August 25, 1727, there were 24 men and 24 women who covenanted to pray around the clock.

This was the beginning of what would become 100 years of continuous prayer! The Moravians began to experience the greater things as they flowed in the gifts of the Spirit, including prophesy and healing. Five years later, they sent out their first missionaries. The Moravians possessed a "fervent revival zeal for foreign missions that took them into various parts of continental Europe, England, America, the West Indies, Greenland, South America, Africa, and Labrador."[97] Only a few years into this season of extraordinary prayer there emerged the First Great Awakening in 1738, creating a mighty wave of revival that would shape modern history.

America's "Hour of Prayer": 1857-1858

The Prayer Revival that I mentioned earlier marked the United States in 1857-1858 with one of the greatest demonstrations of extraordinary prayer in church history. This move of God emerged after a noted period of decline in the American Church from 1845 to 1855. Factors including the heated controversy surrounding slavery, pocketsof apocalyptic extremism, and economic booms followed by a financial crash contributed to the spiritual dryness of the American homeland. So it was that a time of distress and darkness preceded an outbreak of the Holy Spirit.[98]

In the summer of 1857, a businessman named Jeremiah Lanphier was appointed as a layman "City Missionary" in downtown New York by the Dutch Reformed North Church. Lanphier had gotten saved 15 years earlier in Charles Finney's church, and he was now enlisted to help boost a depleted church membership in the downtown area. His first course of action was to start a weekly prayer meeting "intended to give merchants, mechanics, clerks, strangers and business men generally an opportunity to stop and call upon God."[99]

On September 23, 1857, the first noontime prayer meeting took place in Lanphier's church on Fulton Street with six attendees. That number jumped to 40 the first week of October, and the meeting time was then switched from weekly to daily. J. Edwin Orr notes the remarkable timing of the New Yorkers' call to prayer:

> "In the same week, the extraordinary revival of religion swept the city of Hamilton in faraway Canada. In the second week of October, the great financial panic of that year reached a crisis and prostrated business everywhere. It is impossible not to connect the three events, for in them was demonstrated the need of religious revival, the means by which to accomplish it, and the provision of divine grace to meet the situation."[100]

At the start of 1858, New York City had a population of 800,000, many of whom were Evangelical believers. The move of the Spirit was on the rise among the communities in New York, increasing the number of intercessors on Fulton Street, as well as in surrounding regions of the Northeast where dramatic conversions took place. As secular newspapers caught wind of the emerging revival, they publicized each new development of the movement. Take for instance this excerpt from a February 1858 issue of the New York *Daily Tribune*:

"Some two or three years ago, a daily-prayer meeting was started in the lower portion of the city, which met from 12 to 1 o'clock p.m. with a view to giving merchants and merchants' clerks an opportunity of uniting in acknowledgement of their obligation to Divine grace and mercy. A few months ago, after a long silence, this meeting was revived... and has been crowded every day since the commencement of the financial panic... We understand that arrangements are being made for the establishment of one or two additional meetings in the upper portion of the city, and soon the striking of the five bells at 12 o'clock will be generally known as the signal for the 'Hour of Prayer.'"[101]

In just six short months, the Fulton Street prayer meeting had created such a stir that 10,000 businessmen were gathering every day to pray across the city.[102] In February 1858 it was observed that New York's active intercessors numbered in the tens of thousands. Crowds were flooding the city's downtown churches, and droves of people packed themselves like sardines into public meeting places like theaters and barrooms—just to pray.

By March, other large cities in the Northeastern states had also answered the call to prayer. In Philadelphia there were 6,000 strong coming together for daily prayer, and Washington, D.C. had multiple thousands more faithfully interceding.[103] Boston was another epicenter for extraordinary prayer, with Charles Finney at the center of the action. Along with the surge in prayer came a sharp rise in salvations. New York City alone saw 50,000 souls come to Christ in the month of May. While the New York metropolis got most of the publicity, "the phenomenon of packed churches and startling salvations was noted everywhere" across the United States.

> "Undoubtedly the greatest revival in New York's colourful history was sweeping through the city, and it was of such an order to make the whole nation curious. There was no fanaticism, no hysteria, simply an incredible movement of people to pray. The services were not given over to preaching. Instead anyone was free to pray!"[105]

Between 1857 to 1859, America was swept into a season of extraordinary prayer, and 2 million souls came into the Kingdom as a result. The contagious effects of revival could not be contained within North America; the move of the Spirit soon made landfall in Europe and continued to spread across the globe.[106]

Prayers Birthed in Revival

In modern history, another example I can think of is the Argentine Revival. In 1991, my covenant brother Lou Engle and I traveled to Resistencia, Argentina, a city of over 300,000. In Resistencia there were 65 evangelical pastors who would gather for weekly prayer. After three years of praying, they had invited the evangelist Carlos Annacondia, and 60,000 came to Christ in a 40-day period. Churches went from 300 to 3,000 overnight.

When Lou and I visited Argentina, we had a powerful God encounter. The Holy Spirit moved upon us in such a way that we stayed up until 2:30 a.m. repenting of the sins of sectarianism and separatism in the Church. When we came back to the States, I openly repented before my church, and we took up a prophetic offering for the churches in Pasadena. We then started a weekly pastors prayer meeting that birthed our nightly revival services of 1995.

In 1996, Lou inaugurated 24 hours of prayer that would last until

1999. All the pastors and leaders were assigned a three-hour slot to pray once a week, around the clock, for revival. We truly thank God and give Him praise for the spirit of prayer that was upon our church in that season. But even now, God wants us to revive our corporate prayer life as we continue moving forward!

"TheCall" to Extraordinary Prayer

I reached the stage on the National Mall in Washington, D.C. at 5:30 a.m. The date was September 2, 2000, and Lou Engle and I were preparing for the inaugural event of TheCall. Although it was still dark outside, I quickly learned that more than 270,000 people had already gathered to fast and pray for revival—and there were thousands more on their way. A chill went up my spine as I realized the enormity of what God was doing!

Something shifted in the heavenlies that day as more than 400,000 united in a historic solemn assembly at our nation's capital. During the next three years, I would go on to serve as president of TheCall, collaborating with my associate pastor Lou to pursue his vision of mobilizing America's youth en masse to contend for revival. (I write more about the ripple effects of TheCall in my book *Say Goodbye to Powerless Christianity*.)

I still carry the same vision and passion for revival as if The Call D.C. was just yesterday. For the past two decades, we have had this incredible stream of mass prayer and fasting, with thousands gathering in a unified appeal to heaven. Is it possible that all of the prayers and intercessions have been stored in bowls in heaven that are ready to be poured out on the earth?

Praying into a Season of Revival

I believe that the decade we now find ourselves in, the 2020s, will be a decade of revival. The Church is being called to move forward and cultivate a lifestyle of extraordinary prayer. I believe we are to take action—on our knees in prayer—and lay the foundation for what the Holy Spirit is about to do in our nation. We are in the prophetic season of revival.

There is a temptation to lose our fervency in prayer when things seem to be happening sovereignly. On the contrary, we have learned that when God pours out His unmerited grace, we should give ourselves to prayer as never before (see 1 Thessalonians 5:17). Our God is more than able to bring reformation to our land and revival to our hearts. We need to give Him no rest until multitudes are swept into the Kingdom and a radical transformation is seen in all areas of society.

To this end we continue to labor, pray, and believe! In this historic hour, the Lord is moving like never before, so we must press forward until we see the Kingdom of heaven invading our hearts, homes, and nation.

What are you believing God for in this season? Are you consistently engaged in prayer and contending with the Body of Christ for historic revival in your nation? It is time for extraordinary prayer—to prepare for the greatest harvest the world has ever seen!

Chapter 10

RADICAL OBEDIENCE

★ ★ ★ ★ ★

Just as unity and extraordinary prayer serve as conditions for revival, the third key I want to highlight is the power of radical obedience. The great revivalist Charles Finney once said, "A revival is nothing else than a new beginning of obedience to God."[107] Echoing Finney's words, Winkie Pratney describes one key characteristic of revival as the necessity of renewed obedience to what God has commanded His people.[108] It is obedience—or more specifically, radical obedience—that God is looking for as a condition preceding a greater outpouring of His Spirit.

Radical Obedience and Revival in Acts

We can trace the thread of revival in the book of Acts back to the apostles' radical obedience, mingled with their extraordinary unity and persisting prayer. Before they witnessed His glorious ascension into heaven, Christ's core group of followers were specifically commanded not to depart from Jerusalem. These men were from Galilee, so it would have been natural for them to go back to their homes (see Acts 1:11). But instead, they heeded their Lord's instructions and stayed in Jerusalem. Why? Because they had been promised something incredible.

Acts 1:4-5 says, "Gathering them together, He commanded them not to leave Jerusalem, but to *wait for what the Father had promised*, 'Which,' He said, 'you heard of from Me; for John baptized with water, but *you will be baptized with the Holy Spirit* not many days from now.'"

In his brilliant commentary on the Book of Acts, C. Peter Wagner writes, "The disciples never could have become dynamic instruments for the extension of the kingdom of God if they had not obeyed Jesus' command to 'wait for the promise of the Father.'"[109] In obedience to Jesus' word, they stayed in Jerusalem and, by faith, awaited the fulfillment of the promise.

For 10 days the disciples continually devoted themselves to prayer in the upper room (Acts 1:14) as well as praise and worship in the temple (Luke 24:53). While 10 days isn't a very long time in general, it is a substantial amount of time for an extended prayer meeting! Peter Wagner paints the picture well:

> "The agenda of the prayer meeting had been set by the Lord: 'Tarry... until you are endued with power from on high' (Luke 24:49). They were regrouping to begin the process of advancing the kingdom of God, and they knew from the outset that the task was one that required extraordinary spiritual power. There is no indication that they knew up front that the prayer meeting would last for ten days. They

only knew that it was 'not many days from now' (Acts 1:5), so they settled in for the long haul."[110]

Over those 10 days, they obeyed the word of the Lord and embraced the process. They were not only obedient but persistent. Their prayers, supplications, thanksgiving, and praises would not stop until they had gotten what God promised them.

You see, the Holy Spirit is given to those who obey Him (Acts 5:32). This is important for us to realize as we seek out revival in our own day and age. Revival is contingent on our willingness to seek out God's promises and be obedient to His Word.

> "...God, in His sovereign wisdom, has so arranged reality that, although He might desire to do some things, He will not do them unless, and until, Christian people are obedient and faithful in their prayer lives. The whole world has been ultimately blessed because the disciples in Jerusalem decided to be obedient to their Lord and give themselves to persistent prayer."[111]

The immediate fruit of the disciples' obedience in the upper room was dramatic: heavenly wind, Holy Spirit fire, the gift of tongues, an ardent gospel message preached to a multitude, and 3,000 souls ushered into the Kingdom of God in just one day. The momentum that began on the day of Pentecost would only grow, expand, and take new terrain as the world's first group of Spirit-filled Christians continued to walk in radical obedience. The book of Acts recounts many of their awe-inspiring encounters over a span of 30 years as the early Church kept flourishing in the power of the Holy Spirit.

The Welsh Revival: "Obey the Spirit"

"Do you desire an outpouring of the Holy Spirit?" asked the young

Welsh preacher Evan Roberts. "Very well. Four conditions must be observed. They are essential:

> "(1) Is there any sin in your past life that you have
> not confessed to God? On your knees at once. Your
> past must be at peace.
> (2) Is there anything in your life that is doubtful?
> Anything you cannot decide whether it is good or
> evil? Away with it! There must not be!
> (3) Obey the Spirit.
> (4) Confess Christ publicly before men."[112]

If we truly want to taste of historic revival, we would do well to listen to Evan Roberts. "Obey the Spirit," he admonished. These weren't just words for Roberts. They were a way of life, and one of the defining characteristics of the Welsh Revival of 1904.

We saw in an earlier chapter that Evan Roberts and many other young Welsh believers radically obeyed Jesus' words to go forth and preach the gospel (see Matthew 28:19). They took barrooms and jailhouses by storm as they relentlessly told others about the redemptive work of Christ and the life-transforming power of the Spirit. These revivalists were not only hungry for God and passionate in their belief, but they lived out their faith by being obedient to the Holy Spirit. If it meant that they got kicked out of the bar they were preaching in, so be it. They'd just continue the sermon outside!

Even though Evan Roberts was clearly used by God, the revival wasn't about him or any one person. The Welsh minister G. Campbell Morgan wrote in 1905:

> "Evan Roberts is hardly more than a boy, simple
> and natural, no orator; with nothing of the master-
> fulness that characterized such men as Wesley and
> Whitefield and Dwight Lyman Moody; no leader of

men… He is the mouthpiece of the fact that there is no human guidance as to man or organization. The burden of what he says to the people is this: It is not man; do not wait for me; depend on God; obey the Spirit."[113]

The Welsh Revival, then, was essentially a Spirit-led endeavor. The revival meetings were so attuned to the Spirit of God that hours went by as people sang, prayed, and shared testimonies in a completely free-flowing fashion. There was no manmade agenda dictating events—just spontaneity and freedom in the spirit. An eyewitness described the gatherings this way: "There is no preaching, no order, no hymn books, no choirs, no organs, no collections and, finally, no advertising."[114]

In the meetings where Evan Roberts was present, he only spoke publicly when he felt the Spirit's leading. His appeal was never to the natural mind but rather to the heart of men and women—to follow the Holy Spirit, to stay in step with Him, and to obey His voice. The radical obedience that Roberts exemplified sparked radical change in his community and nation, and it went on to create waves of revival that swept the world in the early 1900s.

Azusa Street: The Shoebox Pulpit

Not long after the flames of revival engulfed Wales, the Azusa Street Revival of 1906 broke out in Southern California. Like Evan Roberts, William Seymour was a leader who was entirely dependent on the Spirit of God. His greatness, as described by many, was linked to his meekness, his submission to God's will. As the Spirit led, Seymour obeyed.

Just take this scene from Frank Bartleman's account of Azusa Street as an illuminating example of Seymour's radical obedience:

"Brother Seymour generally sat behind two empty shoe boxes, one on top of the other [which served as the mission's pulpit]. He usually kept his head inside the top one during the meeting, in prayer. There was no pride there."[115] Thus Seymour waited on the Spirit before taking any action. He never presumed that he had the answer that people needed; he always sought the Lord as his ultimate source.

Praying and obeying was Seymour's M.O. Before the revival, he had sustained a regimen of praying for multiple hours every day. And after revival hit, he continued to pray in dependence on God.

Walking in Radical Obedience

Church history is teeming with other examples of men and women of God who walked in radical obedience that sparked revival. George Whitefield was another firebrand who took the Great Commission seriously and obeyed the call of God on his life. During his 55 years of life, Whitefield preached over 18,000 sermons to upwards of 10 million people. In a given week, he would spend up to 50 hours ministering the Word of God to others. The First Great Awakening of 1738 came in the wake of Whitefield's obedience, amongst that of other revivalists in his generation.

Charles Finney said, "Revival is a renewed conviction of sin and repentance, followed by an intense desire to live in obedience to God. It is giving up one's will to God in deep humility." We saw in Chapter 5 that the first phase of historic revival is when the Church is revived by the Spirit of God. Our wholehearted return to God is part of cultivating a lifestyle of obedience to the Holy Spirit.

Church, we must walk in full obedience to what the voice of the Lord is requesting of His people in this hour. In a time where the once-drawn line of righteousness has continued to be pushed back by the world, we must courageously hold to the Word of the Lord like never before.

In John 3:36, the Word of God says, "The one who *believes* in the Son has eternal life; but the one who does not *obey* the Son will not see life, but the wrath of God remains on him." Notice that the words "believe" and "obey" are used interchangeably in this passage. To believe in Jesus implies that we will obey His words.

Jesus affirms this further in John 14:21 (NLT): "Those who accept my commandments and *obey* them are the ones who love me. And because they love me, my Father will love them. And I will love them and reveal myself to each of them." Remember how my good friend Lou Engle liked to describe revival? It is God's arrival! In John 14:23-24 (NIV), Jesus again promises to manifest His presence to those who obey Him: "…Anyone who loves me will *obey* my teaching. My Father will love them, and we will come to them and make our home with them. Anyone who does not love me will not *obey* my teaching. These words you hear are not my own; they belong to the Father who sent me."

Only in the context of obedient love does God reveal the deep things of His heart. Scripture makes it clear that we must love God on His terms. Obedience is an expression of our love for Him.

Obeying God's Word necessitates that we follow His written Word and His spoken Word. Jesus said, "If you abide in Me, and My words abide in you, ask whatever you wish, and it shall be done for you" (John 15:7). Our obedience to God means that we will live according to His decrees, as recorded in the Bible, as well as stay in tune to His Spirit. We are meant to abide in Him, being led by the Spirit of Truth in everything we do (see John 16:13).

Today I invite you to be intentional about cultivating a Spirit-led life. Your obedience to the Holy Spirit is the key to living a supernatural lifestyle. That is exactly what the Body of Christ is destined for, and that is what will release more and more of God's glory in your life and in the lives of those around you. Walking in obedience and in our God-given authority in Christ will empower us to do our part in helping fulfill our collective mandate—to disciple nations and radiantly usher in a Great Revival.

PART 4:

ACTION STEPS FOR THE GLOBAL CHURCH

★ ★ ★ ★ ★

Chapter 11

DEVELOP LEADERS IN THE GLOBAL SOUTH

★ ★ ★ ★ ★

The Kingdom of God is rapidly expanding all over the earth, making this chapter in history not only unprecedented but exciting. As the President of Harvest International Ministry (HIM), a global apostolic network, I often say that our heart is global ministry. Christianity has become the largest global religion, or better stated, the largest global *faith*. (I say that because Jesus never came to establish a "religion.")

Christianity is also the most diverse faith on a global scale. From every geopolitical nation, there are believers in Jesus Christ. Even in North Korea, where it is so spiritually dark, there are disciples of Jesus who are still meeting underground. After all, that is where the Pyongyang Revival, also called the "Repentance Revival," broke out in 1907.

Christianity is not only the largest and most diverse faith, but it is also the fastest-growing faith. You may be surprised to hear that around 200,000 people are getting saved every single day. This is primarily taking place in what is known as the Global South, which includes Latin America, Africa, and Asia. The Global North would include the United States and Europe, what is typically referred to as "the West."

Some people will tell you that Islam is growing faster than Christianity, but that is not true. While Islam is growing faster than mainline denominational churches in the Global North, it can't compare to the exponential growth of Christianity that we are seeing in the Global South.

Philip Jenkins, a Penn State University professor, highlights the Global South in his book *The Next Christendom* as key areas where God is noticeably moving. While Europe and North America were home to 83% of the world's Christians in 1900, the tables have dramatically turned within the last century. It is estimated that 72% of Christians will be living in the Global South by the year 2050.[116]

Nations that were previously totally unreached with the Gospel of Jesus Christ are now exploding with church growth. I have had the privilege and honor of visiting many of these countries to minister, and I have seen firsthand the desire and passion that people have for God. They are willing to stand for hours, travel for days, and gather in tight crowds to hear the Word of God because they are hungry for the truth, freedom, and love of God. And our heavenly Father is responding by touching hearts and pouring out His Spirit upon multitudes of men, women, and children all over the world.

According to the late C. Peter Wagner, there are five hotspots around the world where we are seeing the greatest harvest of souls coming into the Kingdom of God: China, India, Brazil, Nigeria, and Indonesia. Peter was a church growth expert, a prolific writer, a professor of missiology at Fuller Seminary in Pasadena, California for 30 years, and he was my spiritual father and my apostle. Peter delineated these hotspots in 2016 shortly before he passed away, but his statement is still accurate today. It is no coincidence that all five of these countries are ranked in the top ten largest countries in the world by population and all five are located in the Global South.

We have already seen some of the significant indicators of revival in China and Nigeria in Chapter 3. Let me share some of the exciting moves of the Spirit in the other revival hotspots: Indonesia, India, and Brazil.

The Wind of the Spirit in Indonesia

Made up of over 17,000 islands in Southeast Asia, Indonesia has the fourth-largest population in the world. It is also the world's largest Muslim nation—but that doesn't stop God from moving powerfully in revival! Remarkably, some of the world's largest churches can be found in Indonesia. The move of the Holy Spirit is really changing the tide in this nation, as Islam is waning and around 1 million Muslims are getting saved every year on Indonesian soil. According to Peter Wagner, 35% of Indonesia is now born again.

A few years ago, I was quoting that very statistic when Mel Tari was in the audience. Mel Tari is an evangelist who brought revival to Indonesia, and the author of the bestseller *Like a Mighty Wind*. In his book he writes about all the miracles that believers on the island of Timor experienced, just like what we read about in the Gospels— including people walking on water, seeing food multiplied, and the dead being raised.

After hearing that quote, Mel Tari came up to me and said, "With all due respect, you are inaccurate." In the moment, I was expecting him to correct me for making an overstatement, even though I was just quoting what I had heard from Peter Wagner. But it was quite the opposite: Mel said he believes that 40% or even 45%

of Indonesians are born-again believers. Praise God for what He is doing in Indonesia and all around the world!

Barrier-Breaking Growth in India

Among the five hotspots for revival, India is right behind China with its high population density and staggering influx of new believers. This is a nation with an incredibly diverse tapestry of languages, religions, and ethnicities. Out of 1.3 billion inhabitants, today it is believed there are more than 40 million Christians in India.[117] On a daily basis 25,000 people are getting saved in India, primarily in the south.

India is another nation where God has called me to serve, and HIM has a significant presence in this nation. I want to highlight one incredibly courageous mover and shaker, Leanna Cinquanta, who is a member of HIM and the leader of a major apostolic movement in India. Leanna is a leader who has unlocked a major key in seeing rapid, indigenous church growth: She pours into local church leaders and empowers them to lead and pastor movements. The results have been astounding, and extremely effective.

Within the last few years, the movement that Leanna oversees has grown to over 25,000 churches. Their ministry has made major inroads into alleviating injustice in the Uttar Pradesh province in northern India, one of the most unreached areas in that nation. The captives are being set free, and God is moving in bringing justice to India. When Leanna first went to that region, it was 1% Christian. Today it is at 3%. Through one woman's obedience, and the continuing move of God in India, a demonstrable impact has been made in that province as souls keep flooding into the Kingdom.

I remember when Leanna called me a few years ago and said, "Papa Ché, I have a problem." So I naturally asked what the problem was. She answered, "I can't break through the 100,000-

person barrier."

I said, "I beg your pardon?"

She explained: "Last year we led 100,000 people to the Lord. This year we led 100,000 people to the Lord. It's not 110,000. It's 100,000."

I just said to her, "Leanna, that is a good problem. Pastors in America can't break through the 200-person barrier, and you're trying to break through the 100,000-person barrier!"

It's not my intent to make it sound like I'm condemning pastors with smaller congregations. If the Lord has entrusted you with 200 people in your church, you are being faithful with what God has called you to do. What I do want to point out, though, is the disparity between America and India, and emphasize the fact that revival is breaking out in a tremendous way in this global hotspot. Leanna is not only bringing hundreds of thousands of people to faith in Jesus, but she is also training up 3,000 Christian leaders and planting 2,000 churches each year.[118]

Action Step #1: Develop Leaders in the Global South

In this extraordinary season in church history, God is doing a new thing among the nations. The Global South in particular has been home to powerful moves of the Holy Spirit in recognizable hotspots of revival. But let me assure you, an even bigger wave of glory is coming!

However, with a greater outpouring of God's power comes a greater responsibility to steward that revival well. The Body of Christ needs to run with a clear vision in order to embrace the fresh move of the Spirit in this hour. On a macro level, I want to submit two action steps for the Global Church as we anticipate historic revival.

The first action step is to *develop leaders in the Global South.*

If one thing is needed in these hotspots of revival, it is discipleship. As the global family of God, we need to pull together our resources to help our brothers and sisters in the Global South to raise up indigenous Christians and develop them as leaders. We need to help them come into spiritual maturity.

Wagner University: Raising Up Global Leaders

One strategic way that discipleship is taking root in the Global South is through Wagner University (WU). Founded in 1998 by my spiritual father Dr. C. Peter Wagner, Wagner University (originally Wagner Leadership Institute) reflects a new paradigm for unique training in practical ministry. Unlike traditional seminaries, WU focuses on equipping "in-service" leaders with a hybrid online and in-person style of teaching and learning, as well as impartation and activation.

In 2010, Peter appointed me as the International Chancellor of Wagner University, and since that time, the Wagner programs have expanded globally into several regions of the Global South. With programs offered in four different languages, WU currently has cohorts operating in China, Japan, Egypt, and South Africa, as well as international students representing other countries (like Malaysia and Nigeria) in its U.S. cohorts. Wagner is all about seeing the five-fold ministry lived out vibrantly in the Body of Christ today in all regions globally. We want to equip leaders who will make history while walking in their divine calling and strengthening the members of the Church, as apostles, prophets, evangelists, pastors, and teachers (see Ephesians 4:11-13).

WU is continuing to develop new programs expanding its range of bachelor's, master's, and doctorate degrees. Recent developments include a program for Women Leaders and a Kingdom business MBA. The Wagner distinctives—including the Kingdom mandate, the fivefold ministry model, and the seven-mountain strategy—are essential elements of each program. Another element of WU is the focus on producing practitioner-scholars: leaders who can identify the root cause of challenges through research *and* who are also capable of implementing real-world solutions to those challenges.

I have frequently traveled to Beijing and Shanghai to minister and train leaders. Within the past few years, a shift in perspective towards Christianity as beneficial to the economy has resulted in an increasing openness to the gospel, although persecution still certainly exists. As Wagner University has expanded into China, we have been able to touch thousands upon thousands of Chinese believers through education and training Chinese leadership.

Why Discipleship Is So Important

Let me share a story that illustrates the importance of discipleship and leadership training in the Church. To be blunt, I have witnessed a noticeable lack of maturity in some of the nations that I travel to.

Some time ago, I was shocked when I heard that the first pastor in HIM to fall into adultery was from a country in the Global South. I remember being on the board of his church and feeling excited to see this incredible ministry become the fastest-growing church in Nepal. To provide a little bit of context, in 1950, there was not one Evangelical Christian in Nepal. But today, this pastor has seen explosive growth in his nation and even started a school there. So, what went wrong?

The story goes that this pastor was married, but his wife couldn't have any children. Somehow, he rationalized that God wanted him to have children—by any means—so he decided to hook up with different women, trying to get them pregnant. The fifth woman he was with became pregnant, and then she became his second wife. This is crazy thinking!

When all of this came out into the light, my respected friend Cindy Jacobs gave me some perspective on the situation. She told me, "Ché, you have to realize that Christianity is so young there [in Nepal]. We take things for granted because we have hundreds of years of biblical teaching, so our worldview has been shaped by Scripture. But for believers in Nepal, it is all new."

To be sure, Cindy was not excusing the pastor's actions, but she was hitting at something very important: the need for discipleship. No matter your sphere of influence, if you are a leader in the Body of Christ, you need to be discipled and trained according to God's Kingdom values. Each one of us needs to live out what Romans 12:2 calls us to do: "And do not be conformed to this world, but be transformed by the renewing of your mind, so that you may prove what the will of God is, that which is good and acceptable and perfect."

The only way we will stay the course and live out God's perfect will for our lives is to renew our minds daily in the Word of God. This requires discipline, which is the root of the word *discipleship*. It is imperative for us, as the united Body of Christ around the globe, to do whatever we can to implement leadership training for believers in the Global South. By sowing our time, attention, and resources into these nations, we will make a huge difference advancing the Kingdom of God.

Where Your Treasure Is...

Another story that comes to mind took place during one of my trips to Brazil. But before I share the story, let me paint the backdrop for the fifth of Peter Wagner's revival hotspots.

Historically a Catholic nation, Brazil now stands out on the map as a global hotspot for revival. During recent decades, the population in Brazil has increased dramatically, and simultaneously more Brazilians have become born-again Christians, especially

Charismatic. Peter Wagner believed that Brazil would be the first nation where the majority of the population is born again. Right now, more than 40% of people in Brazil are authentic believers in Christ. Brazil is in the midst of revival!

It is not uncommon in Brazil to go through a city and see mega-churches of 25,000 to 75,000 people. I was invited to speak at a church of 50,000 members in Belo Horizonte, Brazil's sixth-largest city. You only have to go down the street and you'll find churches of 15,000, 25,000, and 30,000. It is stunning to see all of those large churches in a single city.

In February 2020, narrowly preceding the global pandemic, three stadiums in Brasilia and Sao Paulo welcomed more than 140,000 radical believers banding together for The Send Brazil—with over 2.2 million joining in via livestream. The Send Brazil took place in three separate stadiums and was dubbed by local news outlets as the "largest Christian simultaneous event in Brazil's history."[119] My covenant brother Lou Engle had joined with various other ministries to organize a paid, single-stadium event focusing on activating believers for the Great Commission. But when registrants maxed out the stadium's capacity within just a few hours, they decided to get two additional stadiums to host The Send Brazil.

As can be seen, the Church in Brazil is experiencing revival. Unfortunately, however, many leaders in that nation do not know how to handle money. If left unchecked, materialism and greed can creep into a church and taint the leadership (see Chapter 4).

On one particular occasion, I was speaking at a church in Brazil with thousands of people present. During the service, one of the pastors said, "We are going to take up an offering for Pastor Ché and Harvest International Ministry." So they received the offering, which amounted to a considerable sum of money. But to my astonishment, the pastor only gave me $200 and kept the rest of the money for himself.

I was saddened and disappointed by the church's leadership—not because I needed a larger offering (the Lord always provides more than enough for my ministries), but because their actions revealed a lack of maturity. The way the offering was presented during the service, everyone in the church thought they were giving money to sow into HIM. But the offering didn't go where they promised. Simply put, the church leaders didn't understand integrity, something we often take for granted. Integrity is something you must be discipled and trained to do. Thus, unless the church deals with character issues in the beginning, it will lead to corruption.

Vision to Advance His Kingdom

In the Body of Christ, discipleship does not just take place on a personal level. According to the Great Commission, we are actually called to make disciples of nations (Matthew 28:18-20). But this does not happen automatically, even when a harvest is coming in. We need godly men and women who will lead with vision to transform their nations.

In the midst of the global pandemic, God spoke to us at HIM and Harvest Rock Church to expand our ministries and launch new initiatives in 2020 and 2021.

On a regional scale, we have been in a significant season of expansion for our church family. During the heat of the 2020 church lockdown in California, we not only reopened for in-person services beginning on Pentecost Sunday, May 31, but we also proceeded to launch new satellite campuses in Southern California. It may seem counterintuitive to multiply your church during a pandemic, but the Lord led us to do just that! While other churches in our area remained closed, we experienced the Lord's presence to expand our dwelling place and take more territory.

The first satellite campus, located in Downtown Los Angeles, was launched in April 2020 with Pastors Gavin and Marlyne Barrett. In June 2020, Harvest Rock Church launched our second satellite campus in Orange County with Pastors Jay and Brittany Koopman, followed by our third in the city of Corona with Pastors Mark and Keisha Anthony. While our campus pastors remain actively involved with our weekly services at our main Pasadena campus, we have been excited to see the satellite campuses grow and expand into new venues during the last year. Then in July 2021, our fourth satellite campus was launched in Sacramento—Harvest Rock's first satellite in Northern California—with Pastors Dante and Darlene Gulino. Most recently, in October 2021, Harvest Rock Church's fifth satellite campus was launched in the "East Bay" area.

The testimony of God's work to expand our borders in this season has been both humbling and encouraging. When we see all that God has done, we can only step back and say, "This is the Lord's doing; it is marvelous in our eyes" (Psalm 118:23)!

1RACE4LIFE

During the summer of 2020, I felt the Holy Spirit stirring my heart in the wake of the upheaval in the United States following George Floyd's death. It became crystal clear to me that unity is needed in the Body of Christ like never before, just as reformation is desperately needed in our nation.

In August, the Lord spoke to me to launch a new pro-life movement called 1RACE4LIFE. Every year, there are 133,000 babies aborted in California alone, making it the number-one abortion state in America. 1RACE4LIFE is a grassroots nonprofit movement of ethnically and culturally diverse members committed to seeing California become a pro-life and pro-family state. With this movement we are passionate about saying, "All lives are sacred, including the unborn."

It is time for the Church to take action and defend biblical family values in our homeland. As we foster a culture of life and strengthen the families in our communities, the need for abortion will be removed. We believe that abortion is one of the gravest evils in the world and often promotes race-centered inequality. But at 1RACE4LIFE, we also believe that the Church has the solution for racial and biblical injustice. Only with the unity of all races and cultures under Jesus Christ will we be able to end abortion and create a legacy of life for future generations. I believe 1RACE4LIFE will be instrumental in transforming the hearts and minds of the next generation as the Body of Christ unites to bring reformation to our nation and hope for life in the world.

During the months of September and October 2020, I traveled to cities in eight battleground states—Michigan, Wisconsin, Pennsylvania, North Carolina, Georgia, Florida, Ohio, Arizona—and Washington, D.C. In each state, I encouraged Christians first to register and then to vote biblically in the 2020 election. I also continued to share the vision of 1RACE4LIFE and welcomed more members into our pro-life movement. Our vision is to start with California as a focal point for reformation, with the ultimate goal of bringing transformation to our entire nation.

I am convinced that the prospect of overturning *Roe v. Wade* is a clear sign of reformation in our generation. While legislation concerning abortion is still in a state of flux, we came one step closer to toppling *Roe v. Wade* on September 1, 2021. That day, the Supreme Court issued an unprecedented ruling upholding the Heartbeat Bill (SB 8) in Texas, which bans abortions after six weeks' gestation. This is a redemptive decision for Texas, where Roe v. Wade was first ruled on almost 50 years ago. I am proud of the Texas legislature for fighting for the unborn and saving the innocent lives in their state.

Let us continue to pray and intercede for our nation, that we may see the complete overturn of *Roe v. Wade* during our lifetime!

Church, It's Time to Roll Up Our Sleeves

To many Americans, the 2020 election was extremely polarizing. No matter your political affiliation, one can see the erosion of conservative values as a result of the 2020 election. I believe this reveals that reformation is needed now in America more than ever before. Perhaps more than anything, the lost election has created more resolve in conservative Evangelical believers to "roll up our sleeves" and get to work in reforming California and our nation.

A critical factor in this equation is that bad eschatology (for example, the doctrine that things are going to get worse and worse until Jesus raptures us out of here) has largely caused the Church to be passive members of society. In addition to eschatology, there has been Platonic thinking or Greek-inspired dualism in the Church that has led so many to believe that only pastors are called to ministry and the only responsibility for everyday believers is to sit in the pews on Sunday.

In reality, there is no such division. God sees us all as ministers (1 Peter 2:9). He expects *you and me* to transform society (Matthew 28:18-20).

Indeed, we are called to be the *Ekklesia*—the Church. Jesus used this Greek term to name the Church (Matthew 16:18) because the Ekklesia in ancient Greece, specifically in Athens, were the citizens called out to legislate and decide what was good for their city or nation. The Ekklesia formed a legislative assembly that had the authority to pass laws and determine policies to protect their rights as citizens. It is significant to note that the title Ekklesia was also used in the Septuagint to translate the Hebrew word *qahal,* meaning the assembly or congregation of God's people.[120]

In a similar way, God wants us as believers to legislate, not only through prayer but also our God-given privilege in the USA to vote biblically. Jesus is calling us, His Ekklesia, to be salt and light in our nation (Matthew 5:13-16). Part of the way we can answer that call is by being active in all the mountains of society—but especially the government mountain.

We see how the adage of elections having consequences is true by the record number of evil and unbiblical executive orders that our current president has shoved down our throats, as well as his attempt to pass H.R.5 ("The Equality Act") and H.R.1, which would give the progressive Left power in perpetuity.

In this urgent hour in America, we cannot back down and remain silent. The Ekklesia is called to shine the light of Christ into society, for such a time as this. We are also called to make disciples of nations (Matthew 28:19). As we help to fulfill the Great Commission, we are to bring Heaven's culture or Kingdom culture to the nations. This does not mean setting up a theocracy, but rather influencing society and bringing cultural transformation. The transformation of culture is part and parcel of the Church's call to be an apostolic people.

Revive California

At the start of 2021, I felt the Lord leading me to gather apostles from all over California to pray and strategize how to bring revival to our state. Following the unction of the Holy Spirit, on February 11, a new initiative called Revive California was birthed as 12 key apostolic leaders from different denominations gathered together, representing the government, education, business, and church mountains of culture. God spoke to me to launch Revive California with the vision to see historic revival and reformation come to California and the United States.

The fivefold strategy of Revive California is as follows:

1. **PRAYER:** *Establish a house of prayer in every church to contend for revival in California and in the United States.* This will take place with all the churches coming together in unprecedented unity. The 19th century preacher and missionary A.T. Pierson wrote, "Before God sends revival, He first begins to mobilize His saints in prayer."

2. **LEADERSHIP:** *Encourage fivefold leaders (apostles, prophets, evangelists, pastors, and teachers) to return and maintain their first love for Jesus.* John Maxwell said, "Everything rises and falls on leadership." We are planning to hold three annual leaders conferences—one in San Diego, one in Pasadena, and one in northern or central California—to help leaders be revived out of their Laodicean slumber (see Revelation 3:14-22).

3. **EVANGELISM:** *Activate local churches in personal evangelism and partner with Ephesians 4:11 evangelists in public outreaches all throughout California.* We are planning to partner with evangelists like Mario Murillo, Sean Feucht, and Jay Koopman, as thousands are coming to their meetings, where we will have the opportunity not only to preach the gospel but also to disciple these new believers in the context of our churches that are aligned with Revive California. Also, through the initiative California Dreamin, we are going to organize Dream Fest outreaches to impact communities with God's love and power. Dream Fest is a family-friendly festival where free clothes, food, and expensive gifts are given away—and the gospel is preached to transform lives.

4. **EKKLESIAS:** *Plant as many ekklesias (small groups) in the marketplace, homes, and churches as possible.* With the launch of California Dreamin, God had spoken to us through my good friend Ed Silvoso to plant as many churches as possible. Now combined with the vision of Revive California, our goal is to plant 1 million *ekklesias* in the state of California. We want to empower believers to start small groups in every sphere of influence in order to prepare the nets for the harvest.

5. **REFORMATION:** *Activate every believer to be involved in the government mountain by exercising their privilege to vote biblically, and also to run for local, state, or national office.* This starts by mobilizing churches to register to vote, through movements like 1RACE4LIFE, and includes encouraging people to become active committee members in their county or assembly district. We want to mobilize conservative Christians who support the same policies that our 45th president, Donald Trump, espoused: namely, the values of pro-life, pro-family, pro-Israel, religious freedom, tax cuts, and government deregulation. We will provide training videos from experienced conservative believers who have seen success in the political world, sharing valuable insights on how to run for office and how to raise money for a campaign.

Dare to Dream

The Word of God says that where sin abounds, grace abounds more (Romans 5:20). For as much darkness that we have witnessed in California, the light of revival will shine all the brighter. I believe that God is going to use California as a template for revival and reformation for all 50 states. This is simply an example of what we are doing, and it can be replicated in any state or in any nation. If significant cultural transformation can happen in California, then it can happen anywhere.

What would this social transformation look like? One major goal of Revive California is to see California become a pro-life and pro-family state. Other signs of transformation include (as expressed earlier) championing religious liberty, advocating small government, being pro-business, eradicating corruption, and recognizing that the Church will always be essential.

All these things can be accomplished by God's grace and the power of the Holy Spirit. That is why we are contending for a massive wave of revival. Now is the time for reformation to sweep across our land—and all across the Global South as well.

If you are willing to partner with heaven's agenda for your city and nation, God will show up in huge ways. I believe Jesus' words in Mark 10:27: "With God all things are possible." Dare to dream that *your* nation can be radically transformed by the truth, power, and love of Jesus!

Chapter 12

RE-WIN THE GLOBAL NORTH

★ ★ ★ ★ ★

T he Spirit of God is moving all over the world, and the harvest is going to come in on a global scale. But I believe it is time for revival to hit the Global North!

In recent years we have been seeing the Church decline in America and many Western nations.[121] As noted in the previous chapter, Christianity was largely tied to Euro-American history until the 20th century, but it has now shifted its center of gravity toward Africa, Asia, and Latin America. Much of the Global North has lost touch with its rich heritage of faith, and numerical trends show a trajectory toward marginal growth (in North America) or an actual decrease (in Europe).[122] There is much work to be done for the Kingdom of God.

If we want to see historic revival in our day, I believe the Body of Christ needs to unite to help re-win the Global North.

Church Planting and Apostolic Movements

Two primary ways we are going to win back the Global North is by planting churches and forming new apostolic networks. Looking to the prospects of church planting, I am convinced that we need to plant as many churches as possible. Peter Wagner, a church growth expert, concluded that "the most effective evangelistic methodology under heaven is planting new churches."[123] That is why we founded the global apostolic network Harvest International Ministry (HIM), which in turn has launched a church-planting movement and discipleship initiative called California Dreamin. Our desire is to see the fulfillment of the Great Commission by planting churches and expanding the Ekklesia into every nation and people group on earth as we anticipate the Lord's return.

We have already seen the extraordinary power that flows through apostolic networks (revisit Chapter 3). To the glory of God, members of the Nigerian apostolic network the Redeemed Christian Church of God (RCCG) have been planting churches in Europe and the United States of America. The RCCG leads the largest church in the United Kingdom, with 15,000 people. Although the majority of members are Nigerian, they are reaching out and penetrating diverse communities with their radical devotion and worship of God. Many Nigerian football players and basketball players are coming into Europe and evangelizing those around them. I believe that these Nigerian churches may be the answer to apathy and lack of passion in what was once a vibrant Christian community.

From what I have witnessed over the years, I want to encourage apostolic networks, ministries, and churches of all denominations to pull together and unite our efforts to reach and receive the harvest. We need to see leaders in revival hotspots—Chinese, Indian, Nigerian, Brazilian, and Indonesian brothers and sisters—plant churches in nations belonging to the Global North. The Word of

God says that we have increased levels of exponential strength every time we work together![124]

Turning Back to Europe

Around eight years ago, I was in England at a Revival Alliance conference in Birmingham when I heard something from the Holy Spirit that took me completely by surprise. "Turn your heart toward Europe and the UK, and start planting churches in the UK," I heard the Lord clearly say.

Strategically speaking, Europe wasn't on my radar at the time. With HIM, my heart has been invested in the work of God in places like in India, Korea, and other parts of Asia. My initial response was, "I just want to do what I see the Father doing, and I see the Father moving powerfully in the Global South. I don't see much happening in Europe, and I don't want to go to where it's dead. I don't have time to spend in dry places."

But as the word settled in my spirit, I felt God directing me to focus on evangelizing Europe and bringing the river of the Holy Spirit to areas that have been spiritually dry for decades. As a result of what God spoke to me, HIM now has churches joining our network in several European nations.

Two notable leaders who joined HIM in 2014 are Dick and Arleen Westerhof. The Westerhofs are passionate change agents and ambassadors for Christ in the Netherlands, where they serve as Senior Pastors of God's Embassy Apostolic Centre in Amsterdam. Dick founded the Coalition for Apostolic Reformation, a nationwide apostolic network devoted to equipping and establishing people with a vocation and a desire to have an impact in the seven spheres of influence. Arleen is the Founder and Facilitator of the Netherlands Prophetic Council, where she trains and raises up national-level prophets.

Through their efforts, and the combined impact of many other leaders in Europe, the work of the Kingdom continues to expand by the grace of God.

Dreaming Again for America

The year 2017 was another turning point for me personally, when God used a good friend of mine to turn my heart back toward the other key geographic region in the Global North, the United States. One cool October day, I received an urgent email from Ed Silvoso saying that he needed to meet with me personally. He told me that God had spoken to him in prayer to personally deliver a word for me. This was unusual for Ed; he is a busy guy, so this email got my attention.

Ed then flew down from San Jose, at his own expense, and Sue and I met him for lunch at a restaurant in LA. Our meeting lasted an hour and a half. By the end of our encounter, the takeaway message came through crystal-clear. Ed told me, "The Lord wants you to turn your heart back to California because He is going to give you apostolic strategy to bring about revival and a great harvest in California."

I have to admit, this was somewhat of a shock to me. "Are you kidding me?" I thought. "There are 400,000 churches in America. Do we really need another church here?" Once again, this was not on my radar. My focus was on HIM and the nations. Plus, I had turned the church that I founded, Harvest Rock Church, over to my son, Gabriel, in January of 2016. Essentially, I had moved on from California.

Nevertheless, Sue and I agreed to pray over this word, and God started to change my heart. He began to shift my focus onto California. I was reminded of my prophetic dream that had brought my family to Southern California all those years ago, anticipating a massive harvest of souls.

In December 2017, by the Lord's leading, we officially launched a new movement called California Dreamin. As we are based in a region of rich cultural diversity, God has given us specific strategies to plant new churches, strengthen and grow existing churches, and increase effective discipleship to bring reformation to society. We believe God has prophetically called us to reach and inspire families, communities, and people groups of all ages and backgrounds in California and all across our nation.

Then in 2018, God circumstantially catapulted me and Sue to take up our former roles as Senior Pastors of Harvest Rock. All of a sudden, I felt this renewed calling to the Global North, even though my DNA and background has been in the Global South. I have been personally focusing on the United States after giving myself to the work of God in our nation. As I shared in the Introduction, the need for courageous leadership has never been more apparent for leaders in America, as our fight for religious freedom through a federal lawsuit in 2020—and the ensuing victory in 2021—required us to take action.

Pursuing the Prophetic Vision

My heart burns with a passion to see a great harvest in California and to witness revival sweep across America. Today, circumstances may look contrary to my prophetic dream, and people could accuse me of having "missed it." Somehow, it's our natural tendency to say that a prophetic word needs to come about in a certain way or according to our timing.

We have to understand that God's timetable is part of how the prophetic works. With every revelation, you need the proper inter-pretation, and along with it, the proper application, which includes the timing. So often we want to be the one who calls the shots, but we need to hear God saying, "I am God, and you are not." Our God is such a good God, and His timing is always best.

This does not mean that I am passive about God's promises, saying *"Que sera, sera"* ("Whatever will be, will be"). On the contrary, I am going after the harvest, and I am going to do whatever I can do to see revival come to Southern California. Since 2018, we have planted 11 churches under California Dreamin. That may not be a lot, but it is more than we had before! Within the last two years, Harvest Rock Church also launched five new satellite campuses in Downtown LA, Orange County, Corona, Sacramento, and the East Bay. We are preparing the nets for a harvest to come in as we contend for the prophetic promises of God over our region.

With California Dreamin, our vision is to plant 10,000 apostolic HIM churches by 2050 that are committed to global revival and social transformation. I am not saying this will happen in the next 10 years; it is our vision for the year 2050. I am basing my actions on the prophetic words that God has spoken to me, without imposing my own timetable on how I think God should move.

The Lord confirmed the number of 10,000 churches a few months after I had heard it in prayer. I was speaking at a conference along with a prophetic minister who I hadn't seen in 20 years. He was a youth pastor at a megachurch, and now he is the senior pastor of a church in Ventura, California. This pastor knew I would be speaking at the same conference, so he sought God for a specific word for me. When he saw me, he said, "Pastor Ché, I have a word from God for you… It is Genesis chapter 24. You are Rebekah, and you will have 10,000 descendants that will possess the gates of their enemies." When he gave me the number 10,000, I thanked God for the very specific confirmation.

Now, I don't know how exactly that is going to happen. In my personal journey of faith, I have come a long way in surrendering control to God. For those who know me well, I am definitely a Type A person. In the early days, I had a ministry plan, a five-year goal, and a ten-year goal. I had to do everything in the ministry plan that I had made, because I was trained to form a business plan and follow it to the T. But when the Holy Spirit hit me in 1994, Zechariah 4:6 became one of my life verses: "This is the word of the Lord to Zerubbabel saying, *'Not by might nor by power, but by My Spirit,'* says the Lord of hosts."

I have decided to say, "OK, God. You have given me this word. I believe that it will come to pass." Everything that God has done has been through a prophetic word. But I am not going to impose my interpretation of the word and say that it has to be fleshed out a certain way in my ministry. I am fully convinced that unless it is the Lord who "builds the house" (or ministry), we are only laboring in vain trying to make it happen in our own strength (see Psalm 127:1).

Winning Souls

What we need to do in the Global North is to evangelize and win souls through the power of the Holy Spirit. Of course, we will disciple them, just as with believers in the Global South. This heart for evangelism and discipleship is in synch with our vision and fivefold strategy in the initiative Revive California (detailed in Chapter 11).

All Christians are called to be part of the Great Commission beyond just the cities where we live. We are called to the nations. If you are being called to the Global North, you need to step into the fivefold ministry that God is calling you to in your sphere of influence. You need to be the best apostle, prophet, evangelist, pastor, or teacher that you can be, in order to bring souls into the Kingdom. We must all do our part, by the grace of God. We need to seek God to receive heavenly strategies that we can use to advance the Kingdom. It is all for God's glory.

We need a mighty move of the Holy Spirit. It is not enough to have only the Word. The church has honored the Word of God throughout the West, but we have produced some of the most secular societies. All of the Ivy League schools in America were established to train us, but they have become so worldly that we now have to re-evangelize Yale, Harvard, Cambridge, and Oxford.

What we need is both the Word and the supernatural activity of heaven to bring about sustained transformation of society. We need to fall on our knees and believe God for a tremendous move of the Holy Spirit to bring revival and transformation once again to the Global North.

Revived by the Spirit and Power

The reason why I am emphasizing the Holy Spirit is because—I am going to say something radical—I believe the Reformation of 1517 with Martin Luther was a partial revival. There was conversion, no doubt about it. There was a restoration of *sola scriptura*, the preeminence of the Word of God, and the revelation of the priesthood of all believers. But you don't read about the power of the Holy Spirit in the Reformation like you do in other historic revivals. The reason I am saying this is because I have been asking the question: How did the Reformation take off like it did and bring change in one generation, but in the following generations Europe became home to one of the most secular of nations?

During the Reformed period, there was a tremendous reformation move of the Holy Spirit in the Netherlands. In fact, the first church of the Reformation on the European continent was established in Amsterdam. But you now look at the Netherlands in modern times, where they were the first nation to legalize abortion, same-sex marriage, and prostitution. This is just my opinion, but I want to submit to you that it was because they did not experience the power of the Holy Spirit during the Reformation and the eras that followed. At the end of the day, we need both the Word of God and the Holy Spirit. We love the Word of God, but we also need to recognize our dependence on the Holy Spirit. Nations in the Global North need a revival that will honor the Holy Spirit, with signs and wonders and the supernatural.

This is why we must completely immerse ourselves in the river of God! I am referring to the prophetic encounter described in Ezekiel 47, where the angel of the Lord led Ezekiel into the river of God until the river was so deep that he could not cross it. The river represents the Holy Spirit and our allowing Him to have total control over our lives and ministries. When the angel brought Ezekiel out far enough in the river, he was in such depths that he no longer had control but was overpowered by the water (see Ezekiel 47:5).

That is a picture of where God wants us to be: the place of *total surrender to the Holy Spirit.* This is much more than just being born again. You and I are meant to offer our whole being—spirit, soul, and body—to God as a living sacrifice (Romans 12:1) and allow His presence to permeate, fill, and influence every area of our lives.

As we allow the Holy Spirit to transform our lives, we will stay in the realm of overflow, continually receiving the Father's love and giving it away to others. The river of God, according to the Gospel of John, now actually flows from within us!

> "Then on the most important day of the feast, the last day, Jesus stood and shouted out to the crowds— 'All you thirsty ones, come to me! Come to me and drink! Believe in me so that rivers of living water will burst out from within you, flowing from your innermost being, just like the Scripture says!' Jesus

was prophesying about the Holy Spirit that believers were being prepared to receive…" (John 7:37-39, TPT)

Luke 5:17 also assures us that when Jesus ministered "the power of the Lord God surged through him to instantly heal the sick." Is the power of the Lord present in your life, in your home, and in your church?

Get in the river of God and stay in the river! Plunge yourself into its waters spiritually, physically, and mentally. When you do, the Lord can do marvelous things. Be sure to bring others with you!

Harvest Time in America

It is time for the United States to see another Jesus People Movement. I am convinced we are going to see that take place.

We are going from glory to glory, and that is why the Bible says that the "harvest is at the end of the age" (Matthew 13:39). At the end of the first century, there was one Christian for every 450 people. Today, one in seven is a born-again believer, and that is not including the Roman Catholic Church or Eastern Orthodox Church.

It is harvest time in the USA. Wherever I go, it has never been so easy to share the gospel with people. A few months ago, Sue and I were at a restaurant sharing with our waitress, and we asked if we could pray for her. All of a sudden, she began to weep. We told her, "That's the Spirit of God on you. Can we lead you to Jesus?" She said yes and gave her heart to the Lord—right then and there. It was so easy, because the Spirit of God was already moving ahead of us.

Scripture says, "You do not have because you do not ask" (James 4:2). Are you seeking out divine appointments as you go about your week? Ask of God, and you will receive!

I love what God declares in Isaiah 60:4: "Lift up your eyes round about and see; they all gather together, they come to you. *Your sons will come from afar, and your daughters will be carried in the arms.*" In the spirit, we can understand this as a prophetic promise for our generation, that our family members are going to come to Jesus during this harvest. I believe we are in an Acts 13:41 season: "Believe in the Lord Jesus, and you will be saved, you and your household." If you have family members who are not saved, I want to encourage you to claim them for the Kingdom of God and believe they will come to know Jesus Christ as their Lord and Savior. "Their hearts are like vast fields of ripened grain—ready for a spiritual harvest" (John 4:25, TPT).

There are so many prophetic promises for America, and we are contending to see them come to fruition. We are expectant for a Billion-Soul Harvest to sweep across our nation and all the nations of the earth. Contend with me, that we may see historic revival and reformation in this generation!

ABOUT THE AUTHOR

★ ★ ★ ★ ★

Dr. Ché Ahn and his wife, Sue, have been the Senior Pastors of Harvest Rock Church in Pasadena, California, since 1994. Ché serves as the President of Harvest International Ministry, a global apostolic network equipping leaders, multiplying churches, evangelizing, and bringing revival and reformation to more than 65 nations. He is also the International Chancellor of Wagner University, an international educational institution equipping believers for practical ministry.

In 2020, Ché soared into national prominence as he championed religious freedom in a federal lawsuit challenging the unconstitutional lockdown of churches in California. In 2021, the U.S. Supreme Court granted a historic settlement—ensuring the constitutional right to worship for all Americans in perpetuity.

Ché received his B.A. in History from the University of Maryland and his M.Div. and D.Min. from Fuller Theological Seminary. He has played a key role in many strategic local, national, and international outreaches and has authored numerous books, including *Spirit-Led Evangelism, Say Goodbye to Powerless Christianity, How to Pray for Healing, God Wants to Bless You!* and *Modern-Day Apostles*. Ché ministers extensively throughout the world, teaching and equipping people for revival, healing, and evangelism. His greatest desire is to see society transformed through Christians who understand and fulfill their destiny.

Ché and Sue have been married for over 40 years. They have four wonderful, married adult children and the eight cutest grandchildren in the world. Their family continues to grow and expand.

For more information about Ché Ahn, his ministries, and his resource materials, visit: cheahn.org, harvestim.org, wagner.university, harvestrock.church, and revivecal.org.

NOTES

★ ★ ★ ★ ★

1. Thomas Paine, The American Crisis, 1776-1783 (Standard Ebooks, 2021), 7.

2. Victor Davis Hanson, "Why Study History?" Praeger University, January 24, 2022, https://www.prageru.com/video/why-study-history?

3. Dutch Sheets, "'God Will Do it Again' | Testimony," July 1, 2019, https://www.youtube.com/watch?v=GuuOyi-uSsc

4. Blue Letter Bible, "Lexicon: Strong's H5749 - 'ûd," accessed September 20, 2021, https://www.blueletterbible.org/lexicon/h5749/kjv/wlc/0-1/

5. Victor Davis Hanson, The Second World Wars (New York: Basic Books, 2017, Kindle Edition), 18.

6. Kelly McCarthy, "Nearly 16,000 restaurants have closed permanently due to the pandemic, Yelp data shows," ABC News, July 24, 2020, accessed February 1, 2021, https://abcnews.go.com/Business/16000-restaurants-closed-perma nently-due-pandemic-yelp-data/story?id=71943970

7. KTLA 5, "'You are right to feel wronged': Newsom responds to weekend violence," June 1, 2020, accessed July 17, 2020, https://www.youtube.com/watch?v=va7rl5seIXQ

8. Samuel Braslow, "Black Lives Matter Estimates that as Many as 100,000 Protestors Gathered in Hollywood on Sunday,"

Los Angeles Magazine, June 8, 2020, accessed July 17, 2020, https://www.lamag.com/citythinkblog/hollywood-protest-sunday/

9. Charles P. Schmitt, Floods Upon the Dry Ground: Giving Foundation and Understanding to the Progressive Move of the Holy Spirit in the Earth, (Shippensburg, PA: Revival Press, 1998), 90-91.

10. Ibid., 91.

11. Ibid., 92.

12. Daniel Defoe, A Journal of the Plague Year with Some Account of the Great Fire in 1666 (London: Society for Promoting Christian Knowledge, 1871), eBook, 116.

13. John Wesley, The Journal of the Rev. John Wesley (London: S. Thorne, 1828), 72.

14. David Barton and Tim Barton, The American Story: The Beginnings (Aledo, TX: WallBuilder Press, 2020), 241-250.

15. J. Edwin Orr, The Second Evangelical Awakening (Simi Valley, CA: Enduring Word Media, 2018), 16.

16. Fred and Sharon Wright, The World's Greatest Revivals (Shippensburg, PA: Destiny Image, 2007), 27.

17. Ibid., 27-28.

18. See Dr. Craig Keener's landmark two-volume study, Miracles: The Credibility of the New Testament Accounts.

19. Charles P. Schmitt, Floods Upon the Dry Ground: Giving Foundation and Understanding to the Progressive Move of the Holy Spirit in the Earth (Shippensburg, PA: Revival Press,

1998), 100-101.

20. Ibid., 101-102.

21. Ibid., 125-126.

22. "John Wesley," Christianity Today, accessed May 4, 2021, https://www.christianitytoday.com/history/people/denomina-tionalfounders/john-wesley.html

23. Mark A. Noll, The Rise of Evangelicalism: The Age of Edwards, Whitefield and the Wesleys (Downers Grove, IL: InterVarsity Press, 2003), 125-126.

24. Schmitt, 1998, 129.

25. Noll, 2003, 156.

26. Ibid.

27. Vishal Mangalwadi, The Book that Made Your World: How the Bible Created the Soul of Western Civilization (Nashville, TN: Thomas Nelson, 2011), 266.

28. Ibid., 266.

29. Schmitt, 1998, 129.

30. Ibid., 155.

31. Schmitt, 1998, 186.

32. Wright, 2007, 173-174.

33. Daniel Silliman, "Have Pentecostals Outgrown Their Name?" Christianity Today, May 29, 2020, accessed March 18, 2021, https://www.christianitytoday.com/news/2020/may/holy-spirit -empowered-christian-global-pentecostal-study.html

34. Billy Graham Evangelical Association, "70 Years Later: A Look Back at the 1949 LA Crusade," September 24, 2019, https://billygraham.org/gallery/the-canvas-cathedral-a-tent-revival-like-no-other/

35. Ed Stetzer, "The Third Wave: The Continualist Movement Continues," Christianity Today, October 23, 2013, accessed on February 24, 2021, https://www.christianitytoday.com/edstetzer/2013/october/third-wave.html

36. C. Peter Wagner, Apostles Today (Ventura, CA: Regal Books, 2007), 6-9.

37. Ché Ahn, Modern-Day Apostles (Shippensburg, PA: Destiny Image, 2019), 39.

38. Cannistraci, David. Apostles and the Emerging Apostolic Movement (Ventura, CA: Renew Books, 1996), 188.

39. Randall Collins, The Sociology of Philosophies: A Global Theory of Intellectual Change (Cambridge, MA: Belknap, 1998), 3-6.

40. Ibid.

41. Ibid.

42. Marshall Kirk and Hunter Madsen, After the Ball: How America Will Conquer Its Fear and Hatred of Gays in the '90s (New York: Doubleday, 1989), 163.

43. "Final Statement of The War Conference," February 28, 1988, accessed on February 4, 2021, https://rmc.library.cornell.edu/HRC/exhibition/stage/REX023_164.pdf

44. Kirk and Madsen, 1989, 189-190.

45. Roberts Liardon, God's Generals: The Missionaries (New Kensington, PA: Whitaker House, 2014, eBook), 48.

46. Ibid., 50-51.

47. Ibid., 83.

48. Eric Metaxas, Amazing Grace: William Wilberforce and the Heroic Campaign to End Slavery (New York: HarperOne, 2007), 183.

49. Karen Swallow Prior, Fierce Convictions: The Extraordinary Life of Hannah More: Poet, Reformer, Abolitionist (Nashville, TN: Thomas Nelson, 2014), 173.

50. Ibid., 167.

51. Ibid., 173-174.

52. Rowan Moore Gerety, "Evangelical Christianity is big in Nigeria—87 football fields big," PRI, November 14, 2013, https://www.pri.org/stories/2013-11-14/evangelical-christianity-big-nigeria-87-football-fields-big

53. Eleanor Albert, "Christianity in China," Council on Foreign Relations, October 11, 2018, https://www.cfr.org/backgrounder/christianity-china

54. David Aikman, Jesus in Beijing: How Christianity Is Transforming China and Changing the Global Balance of Power (Washington, DC: Regnery Publishing, 2003), 15.

55. Ibid., 9.

56. Ibid., 12.

57. "History," Iris Global, accessed February 2, 2021, https://

www.irisglobal.org/about/history

58. Winkie Pratney, Revival: Principles to Change the World (Pensacola, FL: Christian Life Books, 2002), 13.

59. World Bank. "South Korea GDP Per Capita 1960-2021," MacroTrends, accessed November 23, 2021, https://www.macrotrends.net/countries/KOR/south-korea/gdp-per-capita)

60. Yen Nee Lee, "Here are the 10 biggest economies in the world — before the pandemic vs. now," April 20, 2021, https://www.cnbc.com/2021/04/21/coronavirus-worlds-10-biggest-economies-before-covid-pandemic-vs-now.html

61. Ché Ahn, God Wants to Bless You! (Bloomington, MN: Chosen Books, 2015), 82-83.

62. Blue Letter Bible, "Lexicon: Strong's G1411 - dynamis," accessed November 23, 2021, https://www.blueletterbible.org/lang/lexicon/lcxicon.cfm?Strongs=G1411&t=KJV

63. Blue Letter Bible, "Lexicon: Strong's G403 - anapsyxis," accessed November 23, 2021, https://www.blueletterbible.org/lexicon/g403/nasb20/tr/0-1/

64. C. Peter Wagner, The Book of Acts: A Commentary (Minneapolis, MN: Chosen Books, 2017), 64-65.

65. G. Campbell Morgan, "The Revival: Its Power and Source," in The Welsh Revival: A Narrative of Facts by W.T. Stead (Boston: The Pilgrim Press, 1905), 83.

66. S.B. Shaw, The Great Revival in Wales (Chicago: S.B. Shaw, 1905), 73.

67. Morgan, 1905, 82-83.

68. Shaw, 1905, 45.

69. Ibid., 27.

70. Charles P. Schmitt, Floods Upon the Dry Ground: Giving Foundation and Understanding to the Progressive Move of the Holy Spirit in the Earth (Shippensburg, PA: Revival Press, 1998), 153-155.

71. "The New Rebel Cry: Jesus Is Coming," Time, June 21, 1971, Vol. 97, No. 25, 56.

72. Paul Eshleman, The Explo Story: A Plan to Change the World (Glendale, CA: G/L Regal Books, 1972), 86.

73. "Rallying for Jesus," LIFE, June 30, 1972, Vol. 72, No. 25, 40-43.

74. CBN News, "WATCH: 2nd Day of 'Let Us Worship' DC Prayer and Praise Rally," CBN, September 12, 2021, https://www1.cbn.com/cbnnews/us/2021/september/let-us-worship-returns-to-dc-for-9-11-day-of-prayer-for-america

75. Joel Kilpatrick, "Signs of Awakening," Charisma Magazine, November 2021, 15-16.

76. Ibid., 12.

77. Shawn A. Akers, "Hundreds Get Saved During First Night at Mario Murillo's Tent Crusade." Charisma News, August 9, 2021, https://www.charismanews.com/video/86360-hundreds-get-saved-during-first-night-at-mario-murillo-s-tent-crusade

78. James Goll, "My Prophetic Perspective on Bob Jones' Chiefs' Prophecy," Charisma, February 6, 2020, https://www.charismamag.com/blogs/a-voice-calling-out/44262-james-goll-my-

prophetic-perspective-on-bob-jones-chiefs-prophecy

79. Thomas Kidd, "The Science of Sound: Whitefield's Massive Crowds," The Gospel Coalition, January 8, 2014, https://www.thegospelcoalition.org/article/the-science-of-sound-whitefields-massive-crowds/

80. Richard Pierard, "William Wilberforce and the Abolition of the Slave Trade: Did You Know?" Christianity Today, 1997, Issue 53, https://www.christianitytoday.com/history/issues/issue-53/william-wilberforce-and-abolition-of-slave-trade-did-you.html

81. Robert Isaac Wilberforce and Samuel Wilberforce, The Life of William Wilberforce (London: Seeley, Burnside, and Seeley, 1843), 434-435.

82. Karen Swallow Prior, Fierce Convictions: The Extraordinary Life of Hannah More: Poet, Reformer, Abolitionist (Nashville, TN: Thomas Nelson, 2014), 174.

83. Ibid., 182.

84. Charles P. Schmitt, Floods Upon the Dry Ground: Giving Foundation and Understanding to the Progressive Move of the Holy Spirit in the Earth (Shippensburg, PA: Revival Press, 1998), 159.

85. Ibid., 157.

86. Ronald C. White, Lincoln's Greatest Speech: The Second Inaugural (New York: Simon & Schuster, 2002), 19.

87. Jonathan Edwards, "An Humble Attempt to Promote Explicit Agreement and Visible Union of God's People, in Extraordinary Prayer, for the Revival of Religion and the Advancement

of Christ's Kingdom on Earth," The Works of Jonathan Edwards, Vol. 2, Christian Classic Ethereal Library, accessed January 14, 2021, https://ccel.org/ccel/edwards/works2/works2.viii.iii.i.html

88. Fred and Sharon Wright, The World's Greatest Revivals (Shippensburg, PA: Destiny Image, 2007), 169.

89. Carl Brumback, Suddenly… From Heaven: A History of the Assemblies of God (Springfield, MO: Gospel Publishing House, 1961), 36.

90. Charles P. Schmitt, Floods Upon the Dry Ground: Giving Foundation and Understanding to the Progressive Move of the Holy Spirit in the Earth (Shippensburg, PA: Revival Press, 1998), 188.

91. Harvey Cox, Fire From Heaven: The Rise of Pentecostal Spirituality and the Reshaping of Religion in the Twenty-First Century (Reading, MA: Addison-Wesley Publishing Company, 1995), 58.

92. Frank Bartleman, Azusa Street: An Eyewitness Account (Alachua, FL: Bridge-Logos, 1980), 59.

93. William J. Seymour, The Doctrines and Discipline of the Azusa Street Apostolic Faith Mission (Los Angeles: n.p., 1915), 31, 40, 91, as cited in Richard J. Foster, Streams of Living Water: Essential Practices from the Six Great Traditions of Christian Faith (San Francisco: HarperCollins Publishers, 2010), 124.

94. Raleigh B. Washington, "The One New Man in John 17," in Unity: Awakening the One New Man (Chambersburg, PA: Drawbaugh Publishing Group, 2011, Kindle Edition),

Location 574.

95. C. Peter Wagner, The Book of Acts: A Commentary (Minneapolis, MN: Chosen Books, 2017), 61.

96. Alice Smith, Beyond the Veil (Ventura, CA: Renew Books, 1997), 39.

97. Charles P. Schmitt, Floods Upon the Dry Ground: Giving Foundation and Understanding to the Progressive Move of the Holy Spirit in the Earth (Shippensburg, PA: Revival Press, 1998), 125.

98. J. Edwin Orr, The Light of the Nations: Evangelical Renewal and Advance in the Nineteenth Century (Eugene, OR: Wipf and Stock Publishers, 2006), 99-100.

99. Ibid., 103.

100. Ibid., 103-104.

101. J. Edwin Orr, The Second Evangelical Awakening (Simi Valley, CA: Enduring Word Media, 2018), 18-20.

102. Ibid., 16.

103. Schmitt, 1998, 153-154.

104. Orr, 2018, 23.

105. Orr, 2006, 105.

106. Schmitt, 1998, 153-155.

107. Charles Finney, Lectures on Revivals of Religion (New York: Fleming H. Revell Company, 2007), 12.

108. Winkie Pratney, Revival: Principles to Change the World

(Pensacola, FL: Christian Life Books, 2002), 13.

109. C. Peter Wagner, The Book of Acts: A Commentary (Minneapolis, MN: Chosen Books, 2017), 49.

110. Ibid., 56.

111. Ibid., 57.

112. W.T. Stead, "A Narrative of Facts," in The Welsh Revival (Boston: The Pilgrim Press, 1905), 59.

113. G. Campbell Morgan, "The Revival: Its Power and Source," in The Welsh Revival (Boston: The Pilgrim Press, 1905), 81.

114. Ibid., 82.

115. Frank Bartleman, Azusa Street: An Eyewitness Account (Alachua, FL: Bridge-Logos, 1980), 63.

116. Philip Jenkins, The Next Christendom: The Coming of Global Christianity (New York: Oxford University Press, 2011), xi.

117. Ibid., 91.

118. Ailene Croup, "Sense of Mission Takes Cinquanta from Pine County to India," Pine County News, October 26, 2017, https://www.pinecountynews.com/news/sense-of-mission-takes-cinquanta-from-pine-county-to-india/article_7857e004-ba98-11e7-81b4-3b605f841718.html

119. Caleb Parke, "'Historic' Christian event brings together 140,000 youth — and Brazil's president," February 10, 2020, Fox News, https://www.foxnews.com/faith-values/christian-brazil-youth-movement-president-the-send

120. Blue Letter Bible, "Lexicon: Strong's G1577 - ekklēsia,"

accessed January 31, 2022, https://www.blueletterbible.org/lexicon/g1577/kjv/tr/0-1/

121. Ed Stourton, "The decline of religion in the West," BBC, June 26, 2015, https://www.bbc.com/news/world-33256561

122. Philip Jenkins, The Next Christendom: The Coming of Global Christianity (New York: Oxford University Press, 2011), 1-3.

123. C. Peter Wagner, Church Planting for a Greater Harvest: A Comprehensive Guide (Eugene, OR: Wipf & Stock, 2010), 22.

124. See Deuteronomy 32:30 and Leviticus 26:8.

INDEX

★ ★ ★ ★ ★

More Titles by Ché Ahn

Modern-Day Apostles
God Wants to Bless You!
The Grace of Giving
Say Goodbye to Powerless Christianity
When Heaven Comes Down
Spirit-Led Evangelism
How to Pray for Healing

Find these and more at cheahn.org

.

71795339R00126